Things Korean

by Lee O-Young
Translated by John Holstein

Charles E. Tuttle Company
Rutland, Vermont & Tokyo, Japan

Published by Charles E. Tuttle Publishing,
an imprint of Periplus Editions (HK) Ltd.

© Design House Publishers, 1994
Text © Lee, O-Young, 1994

LCC Card No. 98-87154
ISBN 0-8048-2129-1

First Tuttle edition, 1999

Printed in Singapore

Distributed by:
USA   Charles E. Tuttle Company, Inc.
         Airport Industrial Park
         RR1 Box 231-5
         North Clarendon, VT 05759
         Tel: (802) 773-8930
         Fax: (802) 773-6993

Japan   Tuttle Shokai, Inc.
         21-13, Seki 1-chome
         Tama-ku, Kawasaki-shi
         Kanagawa-ken 214-0022, Japan
         Tel: (81) (44) 833-0225
         Fax: (81) (44) 822-0413

Southeast Asia
         Berkeley Books Pte Ltd.
         5 Little Road #08-01
         Singapore 536983
         Tel: (65) 280-3320
         Fax: (65) 280-6290

Tokyo Editorial Office:
2-6, Suido 1-chome,
Bunkyo-ku, Tokyo 112-0005, Japan

Boston Editorial Office:
153 Milk Street, 5th Floor
Boston, MA 02109, USA

Singapore Editorial Office:
5 Little Road #08-01
Singapore 536983

Translator's Note

In this book, *Things Korean*, the writer attemps to show us how the nature of Koreans is expressed in the nature of the things they create. The book itself is also a creation of a Korean, and thus shows us the nature of its Korean author. It also shows us how a great number of Koreans see themselves and the world outside Korea.

At the same time, many Koreans strongly disagree with the attitudes and notions expressed in these pages. Still, most of those who have read Lee O-Young's works enjoy his vigorous style, and his ideas do stimulate, whether or not we agree with them. His style and ideas make him one of Korea's most widely read writers.

It is because of these factors—his essays' representation of the mentality of many Koreans, his provocative ideas, and the quality of his style—that this book is offered to readers outside Korea.

John Holstein

John Holstein was born in Chicago in 1944 and came to Korea in 1967. He took graduate courses in Korean literature at Seoul National University and has since produced several award-winning translations and continued writing extensively about Korea. After two years of linguistics study in graduate school in Chicago, he returned in 1981 to Seoul, where he teaches at Sungkyunkwan University.

Acknowledgment and thanks to those who contributed to the production of this book:

An Jong-Chil
Bohn-Chang Koo
Chung Byoung-Kyoo
Cree Design Services
Herb Clinic 'Sungje'
Hoam Art Museum
Jihwaja (Korean Traditional Restaaurant)
Jung-Hea Han's Cooking Academy
Kang Soon-Hyung
Kim Byung-Soo
Kim Dai-Byuk
Kim Dong-Hee
Korea Folk Village
Lee Young-Hak

Lim Jong-Ki
National Folk Museum
Oh Sang-Jo
Onyang Folk Museum
Pulhyanggi (Korean Traditional Restaurant)
Royal Museum
Samsunggung (Mt. Jiri)
Samulnori Hanullim
Shin Teuk-Soo
Sung Nak-Yoon (Embroidery Knots and
    Marriage Necessaries)
Yoon Yul-Soo
Young-Hee Lee's Traditional Korean
    Costume Boutique

Foreword

The people of ancient times did not see the stars as scattered individual entities but as elements linked together in constellations. Heaven made the individual stars, but the mind of man made constellations out of these stars. And so the individual stars of heaven are the same stars, no matter where on earth we see them, but the peoples and nations of the world have given them different names and different stories. Where the Greeks saw Altair and Vega, for example, the Koreans saw Kyonu and Jiknyo.

If our ancestors made stories about these stars thousands of light years away, would they have ignored, as we do today, the utensils they lived so closely with in their everyday lives? In the tools and clothing and household items with which they lived for hundreds, thousands of years, it is unlikely that they would see, as we do today, no significance other than their utility.

The chopsticks they used for eating, the sashes they used to fasten their clothes, the ceiling rafters they gazed at as they reclined on the cool floor in the summer—all of these creations together formed a constellation in their minds. The nature of this constellation, in turn, reflected their mind. The things they lived with, more than being objects of simple utility, were the expression of what they saw in life and what they felt about life.

Is it just that the rays of stars come from so far away that the stars have now lost their luster? Is this why we in modern times are unable to hear what they are telling us? The things we use every day, too—even when we do regard one of them as more than a mere tool, it is because we see it not for what it is, but for what we can get from it. We regard it as a quaint or cute piece of handicraft, or we admire it for its value as an antique. We have lost the poetics of seeing the object as part of a constellation with many stories to tell, of seeing these objects together as a book with so much to tell us.

The book which you are holding in your hands now was born of the desire to conjure again those constellations. From this we want to form anew for ourselves an image of Korea, an understanding of the Korean mind, and to regain our sense of identity with our ancestors. The dabbler in folk arts and ways and the one who is looking for something to satisfy his interest in antiques will have no use for this book.

The one who may find something in this book is the one who knows the freedom and joy to be found in reflection on the nature of things, the one willing to devote the entire self to the adventure involved in deciphering that cryptic code which a culture builds from its objects to tell of itself, the one who has the eyes to distinguish, through the poetics of objects, the minds of Koreans in the images of the objects they use.

This book is not one man's work. The author deciphered the code in these objects; the editors compiled all this in their original approach.

As you will see when you thumb through these pages, this book itself is one object in that constellation. In this way it helps us understand the entire constellation. The unique Korean mulberry paper used in the original edition of this book has inherent in it something of what the book is trying to say. The Korean script used to write the original is not just the traces of words; each letter is itself a poetic symbol of graphics with independent existence, each having meaning in itself.

This book eschews the usual systematic order of beginning and end. Because each section is an entity in itself the reader is not required to begin on page one and proceed page by page through to the end. Each section is independent, so that you can begin reading wherever you open it. You might open at the end of the book, where you will find an appendix which offers more information on the topics in the main text. After finishing with the material in the appendix you can jump back to the main text, and then jump back again to the appendix at the end for further reference on another topic you may have come upon in the main text. This book can, then, be read in a continuous cycle. In a word, this is a format which has no beginning and no end.

We have often seen displayed in museums the earthenware crock, or a pair of shears, inherent parts of the Korean's everyday life. The crock, the shears, and every other item we see in the museum are individual symbols of an inclusive code which defines culture in one way. Through that thick glass, though, we can only look at these objects. We cannot stick out our hands and touch them. Those shears, alone there on the other side of that glass, can not cut even the softest fabric, just as we, on this side of the glass, cannot come close to scratching the surface of the cultural code which they hold inside.

This book, yet another star in the constellation of earthen crocks and shears—and kites and coins and all those other objects which fill our daily lives—is a decoded conversation with the co-inhabitants of its constellation.

Lee O-Young

Contents

6   Scissors and Their Country Cousin
가위 Kawi

8   A Hat of Principle
갓 Kat

10   An Intimate String Instrument
거문고 Komungo

12   The Egg Crib
계란꾸러미 Kyerankkuromi

14   The Heaping Measure
고봉 Kobong

17   The World in a Thimble
골무 Kolmu

19   The Luster of Lacquer Inlay
나전칠기 Najonchilgi

20   Productive Sickle
낫과 호미 Nat and Homi

23   Paddy Paths
논길 Nongil

24   Laundry Bat: The Cudgel Tamed
다듬이 Tadumi

26   Friendly Walls
담 Dam

28   A Long, Long Bamboo Pipe
담뱃대 Dambaetdae

30   The Magic Mat
돗자리 Dotjari

33   Rice Chest, Heart of the Home
뒤주 Duiju

34   Rice Cake, an Event in Itself
떡 Ddok

36   Letter of Unity and Continuity
ㄹ Ryul

39   From Twine to Macrame
매듭 Maedup

40   Chemistry of the Millstone
맷돌 Maetdol

43   A Grave's Grave
무덤 Mudom

44   Elemental Doors and Windows
문 Mun

46   Down by the Old Mill
물레방아 Mullebanga

48   Our Maitreya Bodhisattva
미륵 Miruk

51   Sister's Wicker Basket
바구니 Bakuni

52   Pants for People
바지 Baji

55   Gourd of Bounty
박 Bak

56   The Boot Sock
버선 Boson

58   Dreamy Pillow Ends
베갯모 Bekaetmo

60   The Lives of a Folding Screen
병풍 Byongpung

63   All-Purpose Wrapper
보자기 Bojagi

64   A Fan for Winter
부채 Buchae

66   A Most Communicative Brush
붓 But

68   Crossbar in a Hairpin
비녀 Binyo

70   The Farmers' Band
사물놀이 Samulnori

72   Ethics of the Floor Table
상 Sang

75   The Porch's Beams and Rafters
서까래 Sokkarae

77   The Yin-Yang Union of Spoon and Chopsticks
수저 Sujo

78   The Old Straw Shoe
신발 Shinbal

80   Relaxing Wrestling
씨름 Ssirum

82   A Rule-of-Thumb Kite
연 Yon

84   Coin of Universal Tender
엽전 Yopjon

86   A Game for Only the Strong of Heart
윷 Yut

88   Cushions and Bedding That Will Floor You
이불과 방석 Ibul and Bangsok

90   Wardrobe Mosaic
장농 Jangnong

93   The Condiments Bay
장독대 Changdokdae

94   Totem Couple
장승 Changsung

96   The Temple Bell
종 Jong

98   A-Frame: Aesthetics at Work
지게 Jige

100   Living Window Paper
창호지 Changhoji

102 The Roof's Hip
처마 Choma

105 The Silk Lantern: Enhancing the Night
초롱 Chorong

106 An Obliging Outfit for the Lady
치마 Chima

109 Knives and Daggers
칼 Kal

111 The Winnow: Dispersion and Cohesion
키 Ki

112 Dance of the Mask
탈 Tal

115 Taekwondo: Art in Motion
태권 Taekwon

117 Yin-Yang's Cartwheel
태극 Taeguk

119 Nature's Own Pavilion
팔각정 Palkakjong

120 *Tripitaka Koreana:* The Sword Conquered
팔만대장경 Palmandaejangkyong

123 The Wind Bell: Where Fish Swim the Sky
풍경 Pungkyong

124 Principles of Hangul Script
한글 Hangul

126 Oriental Medicine: Healing Through Words
한약 Hanyak

128 The Earthenware Vessel
항아리 Hangari

130 Tiger: Laughter in Brute Force
호랑이 Horangi

132 The Brazier: A Crypt for Fire
화로 Hwaro

134 Appendix

Scissors and Their Country Cousin

가위

Kawi

Among all our utensils is there any more familiar to us than scissors? There is not a household without a pair. East or West, they are one of those utensils most commonly unearthed from ancient burial sites.

Scissors, however, have not been blessed with a positive image. Designed for cutting things, these two blades using the awesome power of leverage both look and play the role of the villain. In that world of the sewing basket inhabited by the thread, needle and scissors, scissors, with their nature so different from the needle and thread, lead an alienated and lonesome existence.

That figure of speech which has the thread following the needle is often used to signify the inseparable relationship of a loving couple, but it also shows the capacity of the needle and thread to unite that which is fallen asunder. The needle sutures the wounds which clothes receive in their much abused existence, and it mends new life into them when they seem to be on their last leg. The thread incorporates the nature of continuity. That is why parents like to think that when their baby, at that special celebration of his first birthday, happens to reach for the spool of thread (placed conveniently close to him for that very reason), he is guaranteed a long life.

But scissors cut things which are whole, and sever those which are joined together. Scissors signify to us separation, severance and elimination.

To the writer, scissors are the most fearsome of all our devices. In Korean we say censored writing has been scissored. In addition to their figurative role as the greatest enemy of the freedom of expression, in the West scissors are used as a simile for plagiarism. Imagine one writer scissoring out a useful part of another's writing, then fitting it into his own. Scissors, not the pen, plagiarize. And so we have the true story of how, on the opening night of a play by the nineteenth-century writer Alexander Dumas, the author's rivals sent him a pair of scissors instead of the usual bouquet of flowers. (Wherefore Dumas announced to his audience, "Anyone who thinks he can write a play like this can have these scissors!", to which the audience responded delightedly with a vindicating round of applause.)

In Korean, we refer to the negative mark X as scissors, not only because of the shared meaning of the two, but also because of the strong resemblance between them in form.

There is another, happier image of scissors to be found in their country cousin, the shears of the taffy man. Clanking his huge shears, he makes the rounds of the neighborhood with his white twists and tan slabs, pieces of which he exchanges with the kids for whatever discarded goods they can scrounge for him. Those shears with their dull, loose blades do not look like they could cut a thing, and, indeed, can not. The taffy man long ago scissored the scissoring function out of these emasculated scissors, since he did not use them for their original function of cutting but simply to help sound his arrival. In that transformation from severing to serving, scissors were transformed from the role of villain to that of the much loved hero in children's tales and childhood memories.

Both scissors and shears work on the principle of leverage, but the taffy man's use of leverage has nothing to do with force. When the shears' lever-like blades meet, a lyrical sound, not destructive force, is produced. Those glinting blades of scissors with exact fit could never produce such a welcome sound as the jangling clank of the taffy man's shears. Only the loose, amiable blades of this artless and guilelessly dull work of gray steel can. Shears do not sever; they gather the children from around the neighborhood, unite like thread and needle.

The taffy man is no longer to be seen in the big cities these days. But still we hear the genial clank of his shears in our dreams.

It is not the horrifying quiet snip of scissors that you might hear in one of those dreams which Freud tells us originate in some subliminal castration complex. It is rather a sound which recalls the warm affection the taffy man stuffed into the extra chunks he always gave us.

A Hat of Principle

갓

Kat

That which best manifests the nature of a building is its roof. Likewise, of all the different clothes man wears, that which best expresses the character of the person wearing it is the hat.

Both the roof and the hat are at the summit, closest to the sky, and both of them serve the purpose of protecting us from sun and rain. Let us turn it around once: the roof is the building's hat, the hat is a person's roof.

One architect even theorized that a roof in any one culture closely resembles the hats worn by the people of that culture. There is no difference between the turban of the Moslem and the onion-shaped roof of his mosque. And in European culture that hat worn by Napoleon's troops recalls to us the classical triangular stone roof supported by its rows of pillars.

Anyone who sees the undulating eaves of the Korean thatch-roof house sees in them the floppy brim of the reed hat worn by our travelers in the old days. Our point may be made even more clear if we suggest a juxtaposition of the reed hat and the thatch-roof house with the sombre head gear of the patrician class—the *kat*—and the dignified tile-roof buildings of that class.

Korea's version of Confucianism, which came to dominate our society from the end of the fourteenth century, gave the kat a feature unique among hats of the world. While it resembles a roof, it does not serve the roof's function of protecting. From a practical point of view, on the face of this earth there is nothing more impractical than the kat. This headpiece, woven in a very loose and airy warp and woof from the hairs of the horse's tail, stops neither rain nor sun nor wind nor cold. In truth, a much more attractive aspect of this wondrous hat which, for all its lack of protection, one can wear without actually wearing, is the way it shows off the head under it. The topknot and the horsehair band inside are silhouetted as clearly as the form in a lace curtain window.

This is not to say, though, that the kat is for ornament. On the kat you see neither the resplendent gems nor the brilliant colors of great wealth or high authority. This black kat, even when worn at its usual casual tilt, is the ultimate expression of moderation and restraint.

But this is not to say that the kat is anything ponderous or oppressive, like some helmet or ceremonial hat designed to maintain a Spartan or sublime frame of mind. On the contrary, the unique feature of the kat, more than anything, is in its feeling of lightness. We might say it is the lightest of all hats known to us.

The kat is used neither for practical reasons nor for ornamentation. The act of wearing the kat, and the kind one wears, expresses an idea, a spirit, and identifies the one wearing it. We have the adage, "Put on your kat and await your doom." This means that the kat bares to all the world your self, your mind and soul. Since the beginning of the Chosun Dynasty in the fourteenth century, the kat has announced the social position and the activity of the one wearing it.

In the nineteenth-century social critique, *The Legend of Ho Saeng*, we find an episode in which the hero tries to corner the market on the kat so that he can at least temporarily deprive the aristocrats and Confucian scholars of their mark of distinction, by which, in turn, he hoped to excise the problems inherent in the strict formalism of Confucianism. With this episode the author seemingly denounced not only Confucianism but the kat along with it. Rather than this being any insult to the kat, though, he inadvertently highlighted the kat's moral power.

The kat's message is manifest in the firm and straight consistency of the hair of the horse's tail. It is soft, not hard like steel. The kat's silken black sheen nevertheless manifests the strict integrity it attests to. The material is itself the embodiment of the Korean spirit.

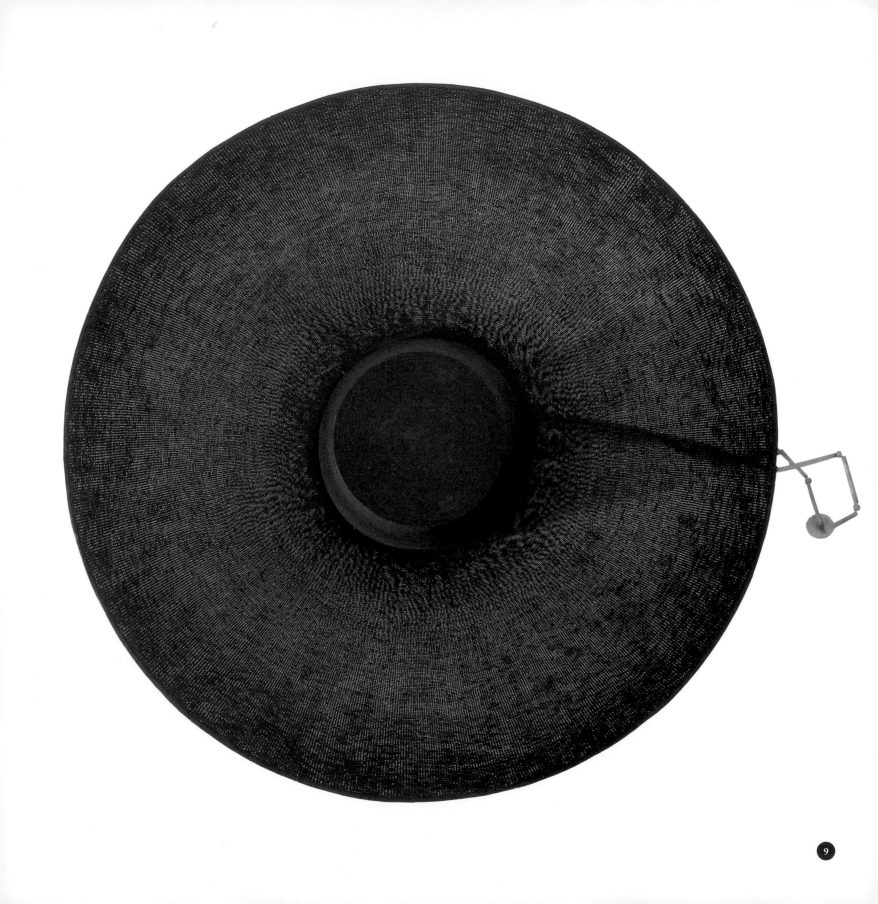

An Intimate String Instrument
거문고
Komungo

The distinctive nature of every musical instrument is manifested more in how it produces sound than in the sound it produces.

No matter how beautiful or peaceful the music from Western culture's musical instruments can sometimes be, one cannot escape the fact that these instruments have an aggressive character. The piano separates the performer from his audience and, despite the fact that it is a string instrument, is played like a percussion instrument, in that the performer has to beat on its keyboard. The performer assumes an attitude of confrontation with his instrument. The same goes for the violin, in spite of the fact that the performer almost hugs it to himself. Observe a bit more closely how it is held in performance, and you will get the impression that some bird in the act of flying off into the blue has been caught in one hand, stuck up under the chin, and with the other hand is simultaneously being sawed in half and plucked of its feathers.

The western instrument which seems to be most intimate with its human performer is the guitar. In both its timbre and in its role

it is different from the instruments of soloist recitals. At countless campfires and parties and other social gatherings its congenial strains serve to bring all together in a communal spirit. It also shows great intimacy with its master, cradled as it is in his lap while he is playing it.

But even the guitar, in comparison with the Korean *komunko*, cannot completely shed the character of confrontation and aggressiveness. The guitar is grasped at its neck, and set up in the lap; the komunko, on the other hand, is not grasped or clutched anywhere, and is in a fully reclining position, rested across one's crossed legs. There is not the slightest hint of con-

frontation or aggression in the movement of the person playing the komunko. In the performer, left hand pressing the chords and right hand working the bow, we see a mother stroking her sleeping baby, or one straightening the cover of the sleeping lover. On another occasion you will glimpse one feeling the brow of a sick friend, or another rinsing his hands in a flowing brook. If the Westerner were to see the komunko in action, he might see the Pieta, Mary grieving over the lifeless body of the son on her lap. There is no sense of confrontation or struggle between the komunko and the musician playing it. They are the most intimate of friends.

In action, all musical instruments either stand erect by themselves or are propped up with something. As a rule, they produce sound when they are erect, and fall into

silence when they are resting back in recline. But when an instrument assumes that erect posture, trying to escape the hold of gravity, its tone is going to be strident. When the violin is hitting its high notes, its song and the gestures of the one playing it shoot off sparks into the sky. And just picture those trumpets of the "Fanfare" reaching together to the heavens.

And then there is the komunko, the one exception to this rule that activity happens in an erect position. The komunko performs in recline, and rests standing erect, propped against something, after it has finished performing. So it is active in its horizontal state, and inactive in its vertical state.

When does the human being recline? Certainly not when he is working or fighting or in pursuit of his goals. The musical instrument, too, achieves its purpose when it is erect.

The komunko, however, could not impart the intimacy and tenderness it does if it were played in an upright position. This apparent paradox in the komunko may be the very reason we feel a real friend close by when we hear its moving strains.

The Egg Crib
계란꾸러미
Kyerankkuromi

The egg is a very fragile thing. Its shell, which gives way at the chick's first flexing of his muscles, is the most sensitive wall in all of life. It could very well be that this fact prompted the adage, "You don't walk along the castle walls with a load of eggs."

Eggs can not sit still, and even a miracle could not make an egg stand on its end. This is where the well-known anecdote about "Columbus' egg" originates. And an egg will go bad quickly. It will turn rotten just like that, if you do not sit there and watch it. Something that breaks so easily, that will not stay in one place, and goes bad so quickly has got to be packaged properly. It is easy to see how the packaging industry started with the egg.

Koreans used to package their eggs in woven straw. That soft, absorbent straw which protected its eggs from shock and moisture performed the same function the

nest does for a bird in providing coziness and security for its eggs.

The fact that Korea's egg crib is made of straw is interesting enough, but there is more. The Japanese, after all, also protect their eggs in straw. But there is a difference. The egg crib in Japan completely encloses the eggs, whereas the Korean egg crib has no top on it.

Why then would our egg crib stop half way up? The Japanese, thinking only of its main function, do it their way to protect the egg. But thinking only in terms of physical function prevents you from seeing the condition of the egg inside, and this ultimately defeats the purpose of the egg crib. When the buyer sees only a bunch of straw, and not what is inside, he will tend to forget how fragile the eggs are. The eggs inside want to warn, "Be careful with us!" but their warning is stifled under that tightly woven lid of straw. So the

egg crib becomes a plaything of functional rationalism, that mighty god of modern industrial society who plays his destructive game with the form and structure of everything we build.

The Korean's topless egg crib accomplishes both the physical function of protecting the egg and the equally important function of conveying information. The one carrying the eggs, seeing the fragile things in their container, is constantly reminded of the necessity of careful handling. But even before the eggs are purchased and carried off, this uncovered container allows the customer to see how big or small the eggs are and what condition they are in.

This egg carton is remarkable not only for the information it provides. It is aesthetically pleasing. In its color, in its geometric balance of straight and curving line, in its texture of the organic and the inorganic, this

straw crib for eggs evokes that sense of beauty one feels in the ideal blend of contrast and harmony which we can witness in the abstract sculpture.

When a package simultaneously performs the dual function of protecting and displaying its contents, it achieves complete justification for its existence.

What we have in the Korean egg crib is the dream of post-modernism, to free mankind from that over-simplification and minimalization born of the West's scientific "rationalism." Inherent in the open Korean egg crib, which communicates with its bearer, is the authentic spirit of the rational. We might say that the Korean egg crib, with its aesthetic form, its scientific function, and its informative display of its contents, is the prototype of the modern package.

The Heaping Measure
고봉
Kobong

Kobong is a concept which has no one-word equivalent in other languages. This is probably because the concept itself does not exist in other cultures. It means heaping the measuring cup till it overflows, and even then some.

When we measure fabric with a yardstick or weigh meat with a scale, we are as exact as possible. After all, that is what a measure is for. So when we measure grain, we are supposed to give no more and no less. That is how the Japanese do it, anyway.

Koreans, strangely enough, inaccurately use this device developed for accurate measure. And they misuse it deliberately. That is how we get the heaping measure. To provide some idea of how high it is heaped, a dishonest measure in Korea is one where the grain is heaped to overflowing only twice, not three or four times.

If it is not absolutely spilling over, that is being pretty stingy. At meals the mound of rice above the bowl is almost as high as the bowl is deep. It is even higher, if such a thing were possible, on birthdays. And when we offer a bowl of water, it has to be sloshing over the brim for the one offering it to feel right.

That conical form of the heaping measure may remind one of Egypt's towering pyramids. But the beauty of the heaping measure is not only in the symmetry of its external form, something we see only with our eyes. There is meaning there, too. That conical form shows that we have given so much extra that we have reached the limit where it is physically impossible to give any more. The heaped cup is the visual expression of a heart with no bounds.

Every vessel has its own limiting capacity. In this way a vessel is like a scale, or a yardstick, made to limit with its own limitations. But the heaped cup shows how the warm heart of a Korean obliterates restraining physical confines and does away with limitations. The heaping cup shows a heart that is bigger than the vessel being used.

A world of scales and yardsticks is not a world dictated by feeling for others. It is a world ruled by rationality. And so the scale is the basis of all commerce, and in this world of buying and selling we demand the exact measurement. The heaping measure is the Korean's attempt to change such a world into one of really human interaction, based on feeling for others. With this, even in the midst of the most competitive marketplace, the heaping measure will bring back the same to its giver.

That brimming measure heaped so high is the height a person can attain. It is that grand stature which comes from feeling for others.

The World in a Thimble
골무
Kolmu

Among those devices which man has made from steel, we might say that the most symbolic contrast can be found in the sword and the needle.

Man uses the sword and woman uses the needle. The sword cuts and severs, and the needle stitches and mends. The sword exists for killing and the needle for maintaining. The sword rules the field of battle, to fight and conquer, but the needle rules in the inner recesses of the women's quarters, to mend and make anew. The sword calls us out, and the needle beckons us in.

In this extreme opposition we can see the intriguing contrast between man's helmet and woman's thimble. The helmet is worn on the head to ward off the sword, and the thimble is worn on the finger to stop the needle. Just as man wears his helmet when he goes out to do battle, the woman wears her thimble when she picks up something to mend.

It is a small and delicate world in that thimble there on the tip of the finger, and the woman arms herself with this thimble to protect that world. It is a quiet world which does not know the male's arrogant hunger for fame and glory. The world which the thimble guards is not a vast empire but one the size of a sewing box.

The thimble is the smallest and lightest of helmets. Like the bits of thread and fabric left over from sewing, like unmatching buttons, it is a microcosm of everyday life.

And so a glance at the thimble can bring back countless nights to us out of our past, like mother sewing with her nimble fingers as she listens to the soft breathing of her sleeping children, with elder sister at her side, learning while assisting. Woman's long nights are lit by the soft glow of the thimble's magic. The thimble is her helmet in her struggle with time, so intent on wearing her down. It comforts her in longing and loneliness, in sorrow, in waiting.

Man's helmet.
Woman's thimble.

The Luster of Lacquer Inlay
나전칠기
Najonchilgi

All sculpture projects itself. It does not lay there on a two-dimensional surface. Even a work of relief achieves its beauty by projecting outward from a plane surface. In this sense, as a matter of fact, the relief can be regarded as the progenitor of sculpture. There is no form of art which requires the bright light of day more than sculpture, because light provides shadow, and shadow, in turn, provides sculpture's third dimension.

A gem is a kind of sculpture, in that it is a three-dimensional work of beauty. The gem, however, wants to hide from the light of day. It does not project itself, it withdraws into itself. In principle, the deeper from the earth a gem comes, the more valuable it is. And even when it is dug up and worked on, no matter what kind of material it is set in, it must be set deep for the design of the entire piece to work.

Inlay is sculpture, akin to the relief, and it works together with the gem to effect a special composite beauty. When the gem embeds itself deep in a work of inlay the total piece obtains the full benefit of the gem, and only with this does the gem fully justify its presence in the work. The treasure chest with its fortune of gems, in fact, is always hidden in the deepest recesses of a cave, or in the inaccessible code of a secret map.

Whether a ruby in the crown of a king or a sapphire in his ring, the gem achieves its value only when resting deep within the folds of its gold setting. If it falls out, all there is left is a gaping hole, which renders both gem and jewelry useless.

The gem has a cousin in mother-of-pearl. This treasure gets its gem-like property from having hidden in the muddy depths of the sea. The mollusk clam which nurtured it does not have to be bearing an expensive pearl for it to produce mother-of-pearl. This inner layer of any mollusk has the nature of a gem. And like the gem, the beauty of mother-of-pearl is not in any brilliance it projects. Its beauty is in the way it subtly suffuses the work of inlay with its soft iridescence from deep inside.

No matter how small the gem, its value surpasses that of the gold it is set in. This is because the function of the gold is no more than that of soil, the gem's original home, in providing a second home for the gem. The lacquered surface of inlay performs the same role for mother-of-pearl. In order for the mother-of-pearl to give life to its setting, the setting itself has to provide the depth of the ocean's muddy floor.

In Korea we keep our clothes in a wardrobe of mother-of-pearl inlay. Its mother-of-pearl, no matter how brightly it were to shine, could never approach, nor would it ever want to, the shine of its would-be imposter glass. After all, it is a gem, and gems have a quiet luster. And so the desire of the luster in this gem is to lie in darkness. When we look at this inlay wardrobe in the deepest and darkest corner of the room, we can see its intrinsic worth. In contrast to a piece of sculpture, in the daylight of open space the wardrobe of mother-of-pearl inlay would lose its special quality.

That luster of mother-of-pearl inlay in the darkness—it is made with Korean hands and is the aesthetic of a culture which cherishes the mother-of-pearl. As the mother-of-pearl is given its luster by the iridescent inner layer of the mollusk, our culture has been granted the spirit and skill of setting luster into the darkness of the night.

Productive Sickle
낫과 호미
Nat and Homi

There is a popular expression describing the illiterate as one who "can't recognize the first letter of the alphabet even with a sickle in his hands." This originates in the fact that the first letter of the Korean alphabet (pronounced, by the way, between k and g) is the same inverted L as the sickle.

In spite of its sharp blade, the sickle could never be used as a weapon in attacking another person. Its blade is bent inward. Misuse the sickle, and it is you, not someone else, who is going to feel its bite. It will act like a boomerang when put in motion, which renders it inefficient, to say the least, as a weapon.

In the West, with its nomadic origins, the blades of farming implements are generally turned outward. The plow, resembling the spear so much in form, would be representative of western farming implements. Considering this plow, it is clear how easily the western farming implement can be turned into a weapon.

And so it is that the West has its "Grim Reaper," the angel of death carrying that dreadful scythe. Then there is the sickle in the Russian flag, which has the dual character of a utensil used in everyday life and an aggressive weapon which can just as well be wielded by the masses in revolt.

Korea's farming implements, on the other hand, have nothing of the nature of any weapon. Their blades turn inward. If the projecting blade of the spear or the sword were turned inward, it too would become a farming implement.

In addition to form, let us consider how the implement works. In the West it is swung outward, like a sword, while the Korean swings it inward. The Korean scythe, rake, and hand hoe are all good examples of this.

Let us look a bit closer at the Korean hand hoe and sickle, which present us with an interesting comparison. From the Koryo dynasty (918-1392 A.D.) comes the song "Yearning," which employs a comparison of the blunt hand hoe and the sharp sickle as a metaphor expressing the idea that, while the mother and father are both parents, the father–represented in this song by the hoe–nevertheless does not give as much love to his children as the mother does. So this metaphor implies that the hoe is not as effective as the sickle. The working part of both the hoe and the sickle is what we might regard as the blade, because the one cuts the earth and the other cuts vegetation. The hoe's blade, though, does not cut as well as the sickle's.

Indeed, there is this difference between the hoe and the sickle; but upon closer observation, we can see it as a difference of six of one or a half dozen of another. The hoe can be every bit as dangerous as the sickle. Its blade, as blunt as it is, turns inward, and a really good swing could wreak as much grief on the foot as a sickle could. Moreover, we could just as easily turn this comparison around: the sickle can be made to appear every bit as harmless as a hoe, for if we were to bend the sickle in at just a little sharper angle, we would have a hoe.

To say that the hoe is potentially destructive, though, is not to say that it actually *is* destructive. On the contrary, it is used to nurture life, by heaping up the earth around each seedling. Further, for any object to be destructive, its power must be directed outward. But the hoe does not do this. It nurtures and concentrates its power by directing this power inward. It directs its power toward the root, toward itself, consolidating it.

Does this mean that the sickle, which in order to perform its function of reaping must cut, is destructive? Hardly. In cutting, the sickle contributes to maintenance of nature's cycle of growth. The sickle is a steel cocoon which shows how a lethal weapon can be turned into a cultivator of life.

No, the sickle and the hoe are not opposites, no more than they are destructive.

There used to be many a Korean farmer who could not see the first letter of the alphabet even with a sickle in his hands. But there was not a one who did not know the fact that, no matter how sharp and threatening the blade may appear to another, the sickle and hoe are, if anything, more dangerous to the one using it than to anyone else.

The beauty of the sickle and the hand hoe is that, even if raised in confrontation or threat, the glinting blade is pointing inward towards the heart of the one holding it.

Paddy Paths
논길
Nongil

Most foreigners when they see the Korean countryside feel they are "looking at an Oriental painting." Gheorghiu, the author of *The 25th Hour*, described it differently. He described his impression of the Korean countryside as something akin to the lines in a work of calligraphy. The reason Gheorghiu used calligraphy to describe the countryside is because he was describing not some mountain scene but the circuitous paths which meander through Korea's rice paddies.

The twists and turns in those paths of the old days reminded one of the scenes of nature evoked in a certain intricate calligraphy of a classical Chinese master. The scene he rendered was a pictograph singing in the most reverberating tones of the village life the paddy paths were so much a part of. Recent developments in agricultural planning, though, have gone and straightened out all those paths.

Spread out a map of the world and you can see, in the way the borders between most countries snake around seemingly without rhyme or reason, that it resembles a bird's eye view of the paths which wind their way across Korean rice paddies. No matter how man tries to draw his own borders, they are basically drawn for him by nature's mountain ranges and rivers.

Look again, though, at a map of North America. You see that long, straight line that is the border between Canada and the United States, as if it were drawn with a ruler. Not coincidentally, inside this geometrically straight line was formed that which is symbolized by American culture, modern-day industrialization. We have at work here the draftsman's ruler, certainly not the calligraphy brush which painted the Korean paddy path.

If American culture was formed inside that geometric boundary to its north, what is this culture that was formed within those paddies of twisting bends and curves? Professor Carl Dohr once said that rice farming can never become mechanized to the extent of, for example, rye farming. The nature of rice farming destines it to stubbornly resist seeding and fertilizing from the air, huge tractors reaping and threshing.... Rice requires preparing and tending the bed for seedlings, transplanting them at just the right time, constant weeding, and all day on the sluices to make sure the rice plants get just enough water. A Westerner witnessing this would exclaim that this is more gardening than farming. And indeed one could say that the Korean farmer is more a gardener than he is a farmer.

Westerners, in order to harvest twice as much, initiated both the measures and the technology to extend their plots to twice their original size. Out of this "frontier spirit" came that which we know, in political terms, as expansionism and colonialism.

Rice farming Koreans, though, if they want to harvest twice as much, simply give two times more devotion to their small plot. If it needs to be weeded once, do it twice, and if it needs to be weeded twice, do it thrice. Rice is a crop which requires sincerity and does not forgive a lack of it. In the same way a calligrapher will put his whole self into the crafting of each and every letter in his scroll, the Korean farmer will devote his soul to every plant of rice. If he does not his harvest will be small, no matter how much land he uses.

The beauty of the paths of our Korean rice paddies lies in the way they form the border of a society in which devotion rules; the irregular undulations in this borderline graphically express the society's rejection of cold functionalism. They define a land farmed by people, not machines.

Laundry Bat: The Cudgel Tamed
다듬이
Tadumi

Some use a knife for peeling an apple, and some use it for killing people. The same goes for any other device used by man—its nature depends on the nature of the one using it, and on how he uses it.

Take the strings of the bow and the harp. Both strings are of the same origin, but one is used to pierce the flesh and cause life-giving blood to flow, while the other is used to pierce the air and cause the most beautiful strains of music to flow. So a person's nature can be defined by the instruments he uses, and how he uses them.

They say the cudgel was the first device used by man, and he used it as an extension of his fist. We can see this when we consider those circumstances in which he uses his fist. Not in love. Not when he is resting in the shade, wiping his brow, after plowing a field. In love and in rest the hand is relaxed, open. The clenched fist is used when we want to smash something into pieces, to beat on something, to strike a fellow being. The human arm was the handle of the cudgel, and the fist was the head of this blunt, insensitive object. How this tool was used depended, like every other tool, on the nature and intent of the one wielding it.

The fact that the first device made by man was an extension of his clenched fist, not his open hand, is evidence that inherent in man's devices and his civilization is the inclination towards some quite nasty reflexes, resulting often in violence and war.

But look at what the Korean has done with the cudgel. The Korean changed it into a bat, for both washing and ironing clothes. When the cudgel came to Korea, women took this tool of aggression from the hands of their men. In using it to wash their family's clothes at the washing rock of a fresh spring and, in the women's quarters deep in the night, to smooth and soften the clothes, our women pacified it. This labor of renewal begins and ends with the laundry bat, the tool that started off as a cudgel.

This is why, when we Koreans hear the laundry bat at work, it is not the cudgel's cries of war and distress that we hear. We grew up with the heartwarming, consoling sound of mother or elder sister working in some cozy spot in the night, and the more we hear the quiet, steady drum of her bat, the more we want to hear.

The solid oak bat on that smooth, glimmering washing rock gives off a clear, limpid sound. Together our women, as if they were playing in a percussion ensemble, drum away on the cotton clothes in harmonious rhythm, now and then varying the beat. Back home later, in unity, in counterpoint, they produce artful syncopation as they smooth the wrinkles and soften the texture.

Yes, fire and water will always be opposite extremes, but if you put a full cooking pan between the two you get a wholesome meal; in just the same way, put a piece of cloth between an organic piece of wood and an inorganic rock, and you will get a lustrous sheen. Put a piece of clothing between a laundry bat and a washing rock, and their three distinct natures work themselves together into a melodious tone.

At such a time this bat displays its difference from the cudgel. It is a child of the same wisdom with which the ancients in their day gathered their swords and melted them down into a temple bell, the wisdom with which we will pick up our shell casings and turn them into church and school bells.

Friendly Walls

담

Dam

In any village in Korea, even the lowliest, humblest wattle and daub hovel will have its own wall around the small patch of land it occupies. There is no way such a wall would ever stop a thief, in the first place because that hovel inside it shows there is nothing there worth stealing, and in the second place because the wall is probably too low and old and weak to keep the thief out. And even if some thief were inclined to enter, he would not have to go through the trouble of climbing the wall. He could just use the dog's door at the bottom of the wall's gate. With the Korean country wall, anyone can come and go as he pleases.

Why a wall, then? The Korean wall functions as no more than a demarcation between inside and out. Regardless of how meager his house, the Korean will build his castle wall and rule inside that wall as if there were his own sovereign domain.

In this sense, Japan's traditional *nagaya* house is inadequate, for it has no walls. The system in Japan mandated that no wall could be erected without the consent of the feudal lord. In Korea, on the other hand, even with its history of oppression and exploitation in the era of absolute monarchy, the one who had his own house reigned supreme over the territory protected by the wall. And so the Korean wall, whether a strong country rock wall, a dilapidated mud wall, or even the wicket fence that looks as if it will fly away with the first strong breeze, is as good as the massive, impenetrable wall of some feudal lord's castle.

The distinctive wall of Korea is the rock wall. This wall has a beauty which is lacking in brick walls. Instead of the standardized size and form of the brick, each rock in our kind of wall is of a different size and shape and color. It is rather because of the difference in each rock that all of them are able to unite into such a distinctive wall. They say the reason the rock walls of Cheju Island are able to withstand all those typhoons without so much as a tremor is that each differently sized rock diffuses shock in several directions.

When we consider the way in which the variegated rocks of Korea's wall consolidate to resist with more strength than can be summoned by the brick wall–in which every brick is uniform–we can understand the reason for the Korean people's strong solidarity. They say the Japanese act together like one brick wall, every one of them uniformly adhering to their society's set of standard dimensions, but the solidarity of Koreans is a harmony of all sorts of individual forms, like Cheju Island's rock walls.

With such nice walls, though, why on earth do Koreans leave their homes unsecured with no lock on the gate or on the front door of the house? The gateless rock wall is a special feature of Cheju Island, but seen often enough throughout all of Korea.

Japanese and Westerners have a front hall in their homes, but the equivalent does not exist in the traditional Korean home. Instead, in the Korean home it is always "open house," where anyone can come and go as he pleases. It is the character of the Korean's home and of his heart that once you pass through his wall, you have a free pass all the way to any room inside of the house.

In the Japanese home it is easy to get into the front hall, but difficult to get any further inside. In the Korean home, on the other hand, it is not only easy to get through the front gate, but into the whole rest of the home.

If you want to understand how the stubborn individuality of the Koreans can coexist with their strong proclivity towards collective thought and action, you have only to consider the walls they live inside.

A Long, Long Bamboo Pipe
담뱃대
Dambaetdae

Korea's long-stem bamboo pipe, the *changjuk*, has got to be the longest pipe in the world. *Chang* means long, and *juk* means bamboo, so you can imagine what it looks like just from its name. In reverse proportion to the western pipe, the changjuk has a tiny bowl, the size of a big thimble, and a long, long stem.

Take a closer look at the Korean pipe and you can learn a lot about East and West. When you consider the importance of the bamboo in Korean culture, it is no mystery why the Korean pipe is bamboo. The bamboo is one of "the four gentleman" who are exclusive members in a form of Korean classical art. (The other three gentlemen, by the way, are the plum, the orchid and the chrysanthemum.) these four depict a certain aspect and principle of Confucianism, the intellectual and moral foundation of Korean culture. The principle which the bamboo embodies is the straight and firm rectitude of the Confucian scholar. The straight stalk signifies fidelity to one's prin-

ciples, and its hollow center denotes humility. In the words of one Confucian scholar, the bamboo, which is neither tree nor grass, avoids the extremes of both tree and grass, and roots itself in the moderation of the golden mean. It is firm like the tree, yet yielding like grass. One classical poet, therefore, said that he might be able to manage without his favorite dish a long time, but he could not survive even a moment without beholding the bamboo.

The changjuk pipe, rather than being made from bamboo, *is* bamboo. In this way it manifests the beauty inherent in the bamboo even more than does either the Korean flute or cane, which are made from bamboo. It is long and slender, just as we conceive of the bamboo, and, with the exception of its bowl and mouthpiece, needs no additional parts to perform its function. It has even gone and hollowed itself out for us.

The image it imbues is basically different from the western pipe, artificially bent and hollowed as it is. Put the bamboo pipe in your mouth, draw on it, and listen: you hear that soft zephyr wafting through the bamboo grove. And the smoke curling from its bowl...the mist is rising there in that grove.

There is good reason for the pipe's length. Our culture is oriented toward the elderly. In the western pipe we have the youthful image of sailing the seas in search of adventure; compare this with the image our pipe conjures, of the elderly gentleman reclining quietly with his long pipe, reciting a few delectable lines of classical poetry. While there is nothing more cumbersome than trying to handle this three-foot pipe when you are out and about, there is no greater joy than sitting at home in one's room, as the elderly will, and spending some time with the changjuk.

A wonderful thing it is for the elderly. He does not have to stir to use the ashtray over there across the room. With his bamboo conductor's baton he can instruct his servant to fetch it. And he has his scepter to brandish for instilling in mannerless youth some respect for authority.

There is yet another reason for its length. It improves the quality of the smoke. The bamboo pipe's long stalk gives the smoke time to cool off and drop its bite. And long before modern medicine ever discovered the harmful effects of nicotine Koreans were eliminating it on its way up through that long stalk. It was obvious to us long ago that the longer the smoke has to travel, the less harmful it will be.

The Korean bamboo pipe. That faint sound of an old gentleman clearing his throat is really the wind stirring in the bamboo grove. And the smoke rising from that small bowl is really this old gentleman's long, thin white beard.

The Magic Mat
돗자리
Dotjari

Everyone has heard of that marvelous carpet in the *Arabian Nights*. To a Korean, though, there is not really anything so marvelous about it.

Originally, a carpet is not something one carries around, and so to hear about a carpet which travels from place to place would ordinarily excite the imagination. The Korean rush mat and straw mat, however, move about all the time; they were never intended to stay in one place. The basic function of these mats is to be rolled up or laid out as the occasion requires, and to fly through the skies of the mind in creating the spot that is just right for its rider.

Probably anyone who can call himself a Korean has had the experience of flying through these skies on a straw mat. When the long summer sun has finally set and evening descends over the front yard, the fragrance from the bonfire protecting us from mosquitoes settles all around like the soft darkness. It is time to spread out the straw mat. At the instant the mat is spread, this yard of bare earth becomes a highland meadow of old central Asia. We see the Big Dipper through the gaps between the drifting clouds, escape the pull of gravity, and there we are, floating up into the sky. And as long as we keep reflecting on those stars up there, this spot originally imbued with the sweat and tears of everyday life turns into a wonderland of dreams and transcendent repose.

The straw mat, which turns a patch of bare earth into a meadow, and transposes a place where people have been trampling back and forth all day into a spot where one can recline in peace, is man's creation for outdoor use. In the same sense we can say that the rush mat, ever so much softer and delicate, is man's magic for indoor use. It arranges the space there according to our changing needs and gives new meaning to whatever spot it occupies.

The rush mat creates space of a very different cast as far as it extends. It starts with the physical senses. When we unroll it the combined scent of sedge and the human body fills the air. It gets this scent from its absorbency, which in turn comes from the firm tree and the soft grass which compose its dual nature.

The rush mat has a synesthetic quality to it, in that its invigorating scent stimulates our senses of sight, smell and touch.

In this one space on the floor now appears a floral design, and when we occupy this space we are in a universe to ourselves. No matter how small this rush mat, the continuous weave design under the flower design extends this new universe to infinity.

The beige tone of the mat's underlying weave blends in with that yellowish varnished paper floor covering unique to Korean homes, and ensures that there is no abrupt break to assault the eye where the mat gives way to the floor, as we see happen so often with the carpet. The tone of this basic weave is as natural as nature itself, so that even when we are sitting on its floral design, rather than getting any feeling that we are going to crush those flowers we feel we are sitting in among them.

The rush mat also offers pleasure to the ear. Listen to that subtle sound that is made when you move on the rush mat. A fresh, crisp sound, like rumpling ramie.

The changes caused in the senses are a result of that change in the nature of the spot the mat has created for us. It is an ideal spot, a small miracle. A guest visits, so we roll out a rush mat—in even the most prosaic spot—and that spot is transformed into a banquet for our guest. At another time, a place of work will become a place of rest. One may be playing cards at one moment, but a change of mats can easily change the card game into a memorial service for the dead.

The saying goes, "Whatever you were doing, roll out the straw mat and you didn't do it," which is a rather oblique and not

altogether positive reference to the way we have of damping the spirit of an activity if we tamper with the original setting in a well-meant intention to improve things. But it does show the power which the rush mat has to create a spirit or ambience.

To a Korean the rush mat and straw mat are a kind of stage, a setting in which we can experience a totally new life. Spread one of these mats over a spot in life stained with sweat or tears, and body and spirit soar off into the heavens. Like a ride on a magic carpet.

Rice Chest, Heart of the Home

뒤주
Duiju

Along with everything else, the image of the housewife has changed with modernization. If we picture our modern housewife near a sleek latest-model three-door refrigerator, we picture the housewife of the old days by the massive rice chest.

There is not the slightest trace of decoration on the rice chest. And we would never associate it with such modern concepts of design as "bright and cheerful" or "sleek" or "streamlined." Its occasional iron or brass fitting is not meant to make it more attractive—these fittings enhance the chest's qualities of gravity and durability. The structure of this rice chest, constructed from solid pieces of the strong pagoda tree, is depicted in bold, straight lines. The only word we could use to describe it is "dignified."

The Chinese characters in the Korean equivalent of the word dignified mean the object appears to be filled to the brim inside. We sense a substantial, weighty mass. There is nothing that fits this description better than the rice chest.

The ordinary rice chest is usually designed to store one sack of rice, but even when there is not a grain of rice in it one does not think of it as some vacant shell. It always looks chock full. There are always those four pillars at its corners which seem to be holding up a massive roof, as if this were some imposing religious edifice. These squat, solid heavy legs descend from the chest like the roots of a great tree. Instead of saying the rice chest has been put in a certain place, rather say the heavy thing has rooted there. While any other household item can be dismantled and moved around, the rice chest, no matter how little is inside, is of a ponderous weight which anchors it firmly to one spot. This quality renders the rice chest that same floating beauty one sees in a mountain rising above the mist.

The rice chest shares with the master of its house that stately unassailable dignity and moral character which reigns over the household. There is no less dignity in the ordinary one-sack rice chest than there is in that granddaddy of all rice chests of the early Chosun dynasty down in Cholla Province, which can hold seventy sacks. Any rice chest is the one source of grain for the household, and where it sits is the symbolic center of household affairs. It is an extension of the bountiful nurturing breast of mother, an assurance that all is basically well.

We associate the rice chest with the housewife, lifting open that heavy lid so many times from morning till night in providing for the family's nourishment. This mother of the old days wore no makeup or jewelry but, in her quiet dignity, had every strand of hair up neatly in place. Her heart was filled to bursting with love for her family, and on that heart she kept an iron lock so that none of this love would be squandered. One sees in the heavy lock on the rice chest the same husbanding of nourishment against times of want.

While the English word risk comes from the Hebrew word for daily nourishment, the Korean's daily nourishment comes from the aesthetic of the rice chest.

Rice Cake,
an Event in Itself
떡

Ddok

Scholars of folk history say that Koreans were eating rice cake even before that ordinary rice we see these days at every meal. So rice cake enjoys a certain distinction.

It is special for another reason. While we have rice every day, rice cake is associated with days on which we celebrate something with a special meal. With the approach of New Year's, or the Harvest Moon Festival (around the time of America's Thanksgiving), indeed any of the traditional holidays, we can hear them milling their rice flour all over town. Rice cake makes its appearance again when sister gets married, and then again when we hold a memorial service for our departed.

Rice looks the same and tastes the same and is served in the same bowl day in, day out 365 days a year. But rice cake is a distinct event. How it looks and tastes depends on the season and on the nature of the celebration. The layered rice cake, made from non-glutinous rice and flavored with young mugwort leaves or the budding leaves of the zelkova tree, means spring is here. And that crescent rice cake made of glutinous rice, filled with bean paste and sprinkled with pine needles, means autumn is just around the corner.

In addition to holidays and seasons, rice cake hosts momentous events. There is the

First Birthday rice cake, which celebrates the miracle of baby's first uncertain steps on his earth. There is birthday rice cake, marking another inch or two and a firming of the skull. And, on the first day of the first lunar month, we also share our rice cake with those loved ones who have departed this world before us, when the spirit of our old country-rustic great grandfather drops by for a visit. As the poet Yi Sang wrote, "Out wafts that wholesome aroma of fresh-steamed pumpkin rice cake, and in drifts grandfather."

Rice cake provides a deviation, the feeling of something exceptional happening, and transports us out of the old rut to somewhere new. It highlights and even recasts memorable events in our life.

Rice cake, though, is not such a special event only for what it symbolizes. It not only uplifts the spirit; rice cake also provides sensual delights. To translate the old adage literally, "Rice cake that looks tasty will *be* tasty," which means that the appearance of a food—or anything for that matter—enhances appreciation of it. Rice cake is living proof that man's senses do not exist or work in isolation of each other.

The designs impressed on the broad surface of layered rice cake range from the cartwheel to the rectangle. When we send rice cake as a gift, we send a deeply engraved personal message. Its message does not yell out in those loud colors of birthday cake icing; it is a quiet message subtly conveyed in the quiet abstract.

Even without these artificial patterns, steamed rice cake takes us into a world unifying the senses of sight, taste, smell, and touch. Take layered rice cake for example, layer upon fluffy aromatic layer, each white layer accentuated with rich red bean flour topping. If you want to know how good it tastes and looks and just melts in the mouth, watch how it disappears among the neighbors. And even if you do not invite them over for some, their noses will lead them to your door.

This layered rice cake is a microcosm of Korea, providing a cross-sectional view of the society we have become over the ages, telling us what we were and are. Our rice cake also rejuvenates us with the spirit to make a new beginning.

Letter of Unity and Continuity

ㄹ

Ryul

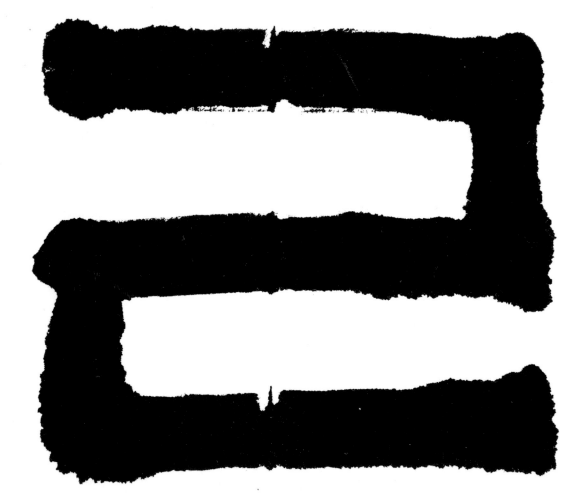

Any Korean dictionary has one section reserved mainly for foreign words, mostly English loan words. Here reside such words as radio, ring and many more of the words we have borrowed from foreign languages. This section is more foreign territory than Korean because so few Korean words begin with ㄹ (which, in an initial position, sounds something like a flapped r). If a Korean word did originally begin with a ㄹ, it has long since been assigned to the section for ㄴ (an approximation of n), because phonetic laws in Korean make the ㄴ come out a lot easier in this case than the ㄹ.

The sound would almost seem to be determined by the form of its symbol. The letter ㄹ is more than a simple representation, a shadow, of its sound; rather, it has a strong independent sovereignty of its own. The ㄹ, with its perfect symmetry, is in fact the most interesting of all the Korean letters.

Korean letters are defined as phonetic symbols. Upon closer observation, though, it can be seen that the Korean system is not just a phonetic alphabet, like that of English. Both systems are phonetic, but there is a difference in that the Korean symbols were not formed arbitrarily, as those in the English system were. Take the English k for example. Is there any more than an arbi-

trary relationship between the letter's form and its sound?

Now take the ㄱ, Korean's closest equivalent to the English k. Its form indicates the manner in which its sound is produced. To make this sound, the back of the tongue knocks up against the back roof of the mouth (a little further back than in production of the English k). The vertical line of the ㄱ is the part of the tongue which reaches from its root up to the mouth's roof, and the horizontal line is the horizontal front half of the tongue. This resemblance between the symbol and the formation of its sound is a distinctive feature of all the letters in the Korean alphabet.

We can see this even more clearly in the ㄴ, the second letter in the Korean phonetic system. The formation of the sound of the ㄴ requires that the tip of the tongue touch the upper inside of the upper teeth, with the base of the tongue in a lower position. This is just the reverse of the production of the sound for the ㄱ.

A discussion of these two letters returns us to the ㄹ. This symbol, when it is preceded and followed by a vowel, is a combination of the ㄱ and the ㄴ, and one more, the ㄷ (somewhere between the English t and d), in both its design and in the formation of its sound. The letter incorporates the

ㄱ's jump of the back of the tongue, and the ㄴ's subsequent jump of the front of the tongue. We might compare this to the number 8, which combines the essential elements of the numbers 1 through 9. The difference here too, though, is that the Korean symbol actually depicts the production of its sound, whereas the Arabic numeral has only an arbitrary relationship between symbol and sound.

The ㅁ (m) also includes elements of the ㄱ, ㄴ, and ㄷ. This letter, however, is closed, fixed, while the ㄹ, with its form so like the swastika design in the lattice window, and with its open-ended nature, affords a sense of continuity.

There is probably no other character which can match the ㄹ in its sense of fluidity. Just see the way it flows and twines, like a hieroglyphic. In this letter so alive with the elemental features of other letters we sense even the soul of the animate object.

A strong dose of ㄹ in poetry will give us a sound and sense of fluidity. If we were to replace a couple ㄹ's with ㄱ's, we would get the sense of something catching temporarily in its course, something tripping on its way. Try it in English: replace the l with k's, and you will see it works pretty much the same way. The difference between the

two, again, is that the English letters themselves do not depict the formation of the sounds they represent, whereas in the Korean symbols you can sense even their sound.

In the ㄹ reside the features of so many other letters in the Korean script, and it is the most aesthetically pleasing of them all. It is truly the Korean alphabet's "symbol of symbols."

From Twine to Macrame
매듭
Maedup

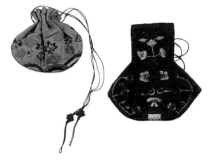

The arrow root and the wisteria are products of nature, but once we cut them off and tie them together they become twine and knot, products of human culture. There are those who say that human culture and civilization originated in the twine. To be precise, twine, like words, was used to signify meaning, and, as we know, for culture to exist there must be some way to convey meaning. The role of twine in the genesis of civilization is witnessed in prehistoric earthenware pottery, where we find patterns made from twine which were thought to bear special significance.

For twine to fully serve its purpose, though, the technique of knot tying had first to be learned. If we did not know how to use twine, this twine would have been of no avail. Therefore it is no exaggeration to say that without the knot the primitive skills of civilization could not have developed as they have. Information had to be conveyed and records kept. The twine and knot depicted meaning as words do. A concrete example of this can be found in the knotted rope used in pre-literate times.

I have mentioned in other pages that the twine is to the Korean what the button is to the Westerner; we can even go so far as to say that twine is the basis of Korean culture. Korea's first twine was made from straw, which was until recently the most frequently used material in Korea. The origin of all our technical skills can be found in the making of straw twine, which was then combined by knots with other twine to make straw shoes, straw packs and straw baskets.

In Korea twine and its knot are not used only for making things. The Korean views life in terms of twine and its knot. When a Korean talks about people meeting and parting he will often express it in terms of twine, as tying and untying, joining or breaking. And if he is in straightened circumstances with no one to turn to, he says in this situation, "my string broke."

On Korean clothing you do not see buttons; clothes are equipped with twine's mate, the strap. Imagine what would happen if our clothes did not have the strap. It would be like shoes without laces, but worse, because the strap also serves as decoration, both in its design and in the way it is fastened.

Twine, too, serves not only a practical purpose but a decorative one as well. The craft of macrame is the embodiment of the philosophy inherent in twine. In Korean terminology the definitive elements of macrame are its nose (the individual knot), its body (the knots knotted together), and its hands (the tassels). Depending on what kind of nose is used, the macrame's pattern can be flat, it can resemble the vine, or it can imitate the chrysanthemum. Each nose forms an empty circle, and so signifies the same as the knot in the strap on our clothes, which is never tied tight, thereby giving a sense of serenity and poise. The body, on the other hand, indicates strength and solidarity, because here all the noses are joined securely together.

The hand serves the same symbolic purpose as the end of the strap on a piece of clothing, which is pulled to open the knot. In contrast to the body, the hand signifies loosening rather than binding, and tells us of itself that, no matter how intricately bound, here is the key which can free. So the body and hand can be considered in terms of opposition, and the nose as their mediator.

The balance of these three elements gives the macrame its beautiful composition. It reminds us of how life is actually an exercise in both the formation and unravelling of relationships.

All activity is performed within the restrictions of time. Macrame takes a lot of time, but it is also an activity performed in space, and so it has structure. Macrame is the depiction of a culture of the twine, and it depicts the evolution and the composition of the Korean spirit.

Chemistry of the Millstone
맷돌
Maetdol

In re-forming matter, three methods are used. One is pulverization, which produces powder. Another is the chemical process of reducing an object to its atomic state. And the other is the nuclear physicist's process of fission, splitting the atom itself. The feature shared by all these processes, of course, is that of breaking into smaller pieces.

When we want to turn an object into powder, we either smash it or grind it. For smashing we use the mortar, and for grinding we use the millstone.

The mortar and millstone gave birth to humankind's tools and culture, which reflect, in turn, the character of these devices. A closer look at the mortar and the millstone will show us an element of aggressiveness. In fact, the mortar and millstone display an even more dreadful aggressiveness than the arrow and the stone knife of primitive civilization. No one will deny that our era's nuclear phobia had its inception in the first millstone of the neolithic age.

Our civilization has found an effective metaphor in the mortar and millstone to depict that element of aggressiveness in life which pulverizes the things of nature. We can see this in some contemporary jargon, in such words as 'break,' 'mash,' 'make powder of.' Chong Mong-ju, in his "Song of

Devotion," mentions, "We know well our bones turn to dust, but we know not wither the soul," thus using a form of powder as a metaphor to depict the idea that our body turning to dust is even more extreme than death.

In addition to the aggressive and destructive elements we find in the millstone, there is the intriguing inference of the sexual act. The metaphor relating the mortar's body to the female's womb and its pestle to the male's organ has been around for a long time now. The millstone, too, with its female top and male bottom, is used in *The Legend of Chunhyang* to portray a deviate position in the sexual act. Chunhyang tells her sweetheart Doryong, "In this life I was the one on the bottom, but in the next life I want to try it once as the pestle, and spin round and round on top."

In these devices' two elements of aggressiveness and sexuality, we can see an important implication in regards to civilization. When that element of destructive aggressiveness acts in yin-yang the union of (complementary opposites) correspondence with the feature of male and female sexuality, there we have the generative power which propels nature's cycle of life. It is not an antagonistic, incompatible opposition but a complementary union.

The fact is, though, that we can no longer find the complementary male-female element in our modern day utensils. All that is left is that element of the destructively aggressive. This is because of the technology developed by modern chemistry and physics. In the era of alchemy, when modern chemistry was in its embryonic stage, the crucible used in combining substances was often referred to in metaphorical terms of the womb, and the chemical transformations wrought by that science were regarded in terms of the sexual act between male and female. With the development of modern chemistry, though, we speak of physical processes only in bleak terms of numbers and arbitrary signs.

The technique of making powder depends neither on modern chemistry nor on modern physics. This technique, rather than being an act of fragmentation, is a preparatory stage in the process of recombination and reforming. That rice being crushed in the mortar and those green peas and beans being ground by the millstone are going through one vital step in the process of the creation of food. It is that same process we see in the conception of new life.

Compare this with the fission of the atom. Splitting that atom is both the means and the end of a process, and it can therefore be considered as no less and no more than an act of aggression.

The millstone in Korea, for all its historical and social importance, is nevertheless one of our more humble devices. Its form and color express this character. Maybe that is where it gets that serene beauty which is recognized even outside Korea.

The Japanese boast of the beauty of the tea house in which they conduct their tea ceremony. One element which enhances the beauty of that tea house is the Korean millstone, which is used in the hand washing ritual before tea.

Korea's mortar and millstone are the antidote to modern chemistry and nuclear physics. And so today do they strike one as a quaint anachronism.

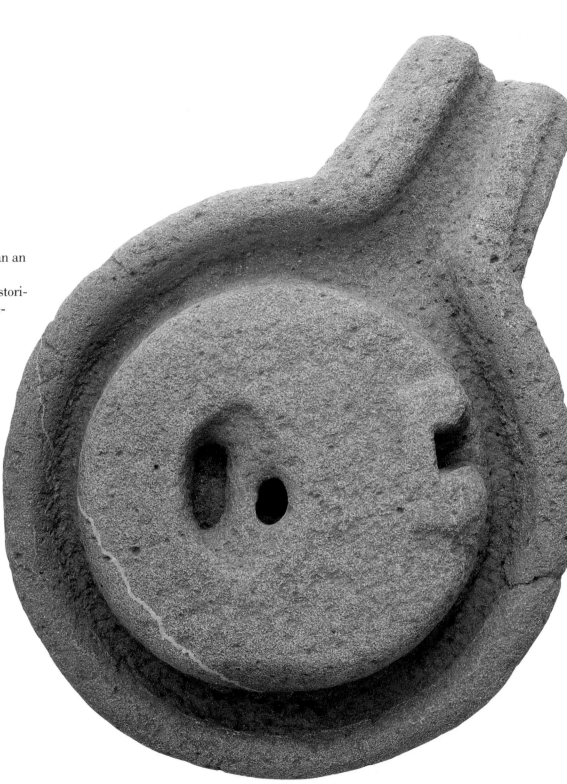

A Grave's Grave
무덤
Mudom

The Chinese character for life is said to have been designed to represent a seed sprouting up out of the ground. And that is just what life is, something which rises upward. There is no event more expressive of this, and no more dramatic moment in life than when the child, who has been crawling on hands and knees till now, rises to its own two feet.

Dying is thought of in terms of falling. It is not difficult to appreciate why the Latin word for cadaver comes from the verb fall. The Korean word for grave *(mudom)* comes from the verb *mud-da*, which means to bury, and so the impression this word gives is quite clearly the opposite of something sprouting up out of the ground.

The Korean grave is a mound, and on it is planted grass, so that it gives a feeling much different from the one you get from the catacombs of the West. The catacomb is subterranean, but the Korean grave rises toward the sky like a hill or small mountain. That is not to compare it, though, with the pyramids of Egypt, which actually give the impression that they want to take over the sky. Even though the pyramid weathers away bit by bit it tries to retain its form, stubbornly digging in its feet in resistance to its inevitable demise.

The Korean grave, however, is made of earth, and over the passage of years lets go willingly and returns gradually back to level earth. So we can say it dies a little at a time. After many, many years, when its resident has been forgotten by his survivors and they have finally stopped visiting, when even the face on its tombstone is indistinguishable, the Korean grave fades back to where it came from.

The Korean, like his grave, does not die all of a sudden, but slowly, bit by bit. Just as life is a process, so is death, and the Korean is in tune with this process.

At one glance you can tell the difference between a new grave, an old one, and one that has been forgotten and deserted long ago. In the spring, fresh green grass sprouts around the grave's perimeter, flourishes in the summer, then turns to gold in the fall; and in this we can see how the Korean, even in death, respects the turn of the seasons.

After many of these springs and autumns have passed, the grass on a grave finds itself taken over by weeds. The cultivated grass at the perimeter of the mound also returns to its wild natural state. Along with the grass goes any impression distinguishing the grave's head and foot. And then before long even the dragon and tiger tablets inside the grave go the way of the body they were left there to guard in its journey to the nether world. Now, not a trace is left of anything that was once there. It is now a grave's grave.

It takes a grave about one hundred years to finally give up its ghost and return back to the earth from which it came. A hundred years to live, a hundred years to die. This is why we say a Korean dies twice.

Elemental Doors and Windows

문

Mun

There is some very nice Korean classical *sijo* poetry which compares the window with the heart. One begins, "A window, make a window, in this heart of mine." Another goes: "One sigh, another; where is the crack letting them in like that?"

Two contrasting functions resting on the same hinge that is a window. A window is that crack in the border of dark and light. If it were only to stay closed, a wall could serve the same purpose. If it were always open, you might as well be out in the vast outdoors. So a window is not this, and it is not that. It can not be explained in strict and sterile terms of black and white; its essence is told more in fluctuating shades of gray.

There are many who complain that the window in the traditional Korean home does not fit its frame snugly enough. No matter how palatial, no matter how well a traditional house here is constructed, that crack is always there between the window and its frame, just like in the humblest peasant's hovel.

Our doors, too. In the West they talk about peeping through the door's key hole, because that is all they have in their doors to peep through. Not us. We can look in and look out around the sides and tops and bottoms of our doors. Even Japanese doors, with the same paper and lattice design as we have, are not really like ours. However poorly built the house, their doors and windows are a tight fit, a perfect contrast to ours, which hang there just about well enough and serve their original purpose nicely enough.

To us, the loosely fit window is the norm. You will not find this window or this mentality anywhere else in Asia, not to mention the West, and so Korea is the only place where you will find a paper specially named for its function of sealing up that crack between the window and its frame. "Window zephyr paper," if you will, has the character of the Korean in it. Even this crack sealer is forgiven if it is not suffocatingly hermetic. And so it is that when you hear the wind whistling through the windows on a deep winter's night, you know you are in Korea.

Then there is the hinge. Westerners and the Japanese have their scientifically fit hinges, and we have our hinge. Our hinge you can hammer in to tighten, hammer out to loosen, and be perfectly happy with the result.

But what does all this mean? Does it mean that we, whose carpenters built Japan's famous temple Horyusha, can not do something just as exquisite here in Korea when we set our minds to it? Maybe our windows and doors do not fit, but can you find any more delicate and refined lattice

work anywhere else in the world?

Koreans know what a window is. They know the secret of the window, that crack in the border between light and dark which cannot be measured with even the most accurate ruler. The one who is able to appreciate the labyrinth that we call life, with all its subtle tones of gray and which cannot be told to the nearest one or two millimeters, is the one who is able to live in the same way a Korean fits a window, the way a Korean lives. And he will enjoy that sound of the wind whistling through the cracks between the window and its frame, a sound so much more melodious than the exacting sound of the carpenter's plane.

The beauty of the Korean window and door is the very same beauty that we find in the contradictions of life.

Down by the Old Mill
물레방아
Mullebanga

In the production of flour there is quite a difference between East and West, in their methods and even in their attitudes.

The Chinese character we use for flour is comprised of the sign for rice and the sign for dividing. The grain which we generally associate with flour, however, is not rice. It is wheat. Rice is seldom ground into flour. It is usually only husked before being cooked and eaten. We can see here a distinction between the basic natures of rice and wheat, therefore; wheat cannot be eaten without first being ground.

So one does not think of wheat without thinking of flour. It stands to reason, then, that when we think of flour we think not of rice but wheat. This was borne out in a survey of 850 Korean students, in which they were asked what came to mind when they heard the word powder. (In Korean, the same basic word, *karu*, is used for powder and flour, and the specific nature of the powder is designated with a prefix on *karu*). Around two thirds of the students reported that they thought first of wheat flour. After wheat flour came cement, sugar, and several other kinds of powder, but rice flour was hardly mentioned.

Korea, Japan and the rest of East and Southeast Asia are rice cultures, and America and the other western nations are wheat cultures. It is understandable that Asians, whose diet is based on rice, fall behind Westerners somewhat in drive, and were later in their adoption of the machine. Those people whose diet is based on wheat had to mill this wheat before they could eat it, and this demanded a lot more drive and used a lot more machinery than would have been the case if rice, which has only to be husked, had been the basis of their diet.

Marx wrote in *Das Kapital* that one could trace the entire history of the machine in the milling of wheat, and went on to point out that an English word for factory is mill. He would have agreed that the West's drive and mechanization came from the flour mill, the prototype of the factory, which in turn played a pivotal role in industrialization.

In medieval Europe flour milling was the monopoly of the local sovereign or the Church, and commoners were prohibited from using the flour mill. Even after the Middle Ages, and well into the nineteenth century, the owner of the mill was a central power in his village, to a degree which a Korean could hardly imagine. The Western mill and the Korean mill are two very different concepts.

The Korean water mill symbolizes neither wealth nor authority, nor is it the precursor of any industrial society. The mill we know is the one where lovers have their secret trysts, such as in the short story "When the Buckwheat Blossom Blooms," where the two lovers met in the old mill to share their first love. When a Korean pictures the water mill he sees some deserted, dilapidated place, not in the middle of the village but in a remote, isolated place outside. In the past, too, it was used more as a place where dreams were made than for the practical purpose of milling wheat. That is because, except on the occasion of a special celebration or holiday, Koreans, whose basic diet was rice, had neither enough grain to grind nor sufficient reason to go all the way out to that mill.

These days the water mill is of still less practical use. It is little more than a relic, a quaint tourist attraction. Maybe we could say of both Korea's water mill, which has turned into a clandestine meeting place for lovers, and the mill of the West, which evolved into the factories of industrial society, that they are relics of the past which depict the fates of these two cultures.

Our Maitreya Bodhisattva
미륵
Miruk

Walking along any country road in Korea you may suddenly come upon a rock standing in the grass off your path. At first glance you may think it is just some small monument or county border marker or such. But look closer, and you will see it has a head and body, and then look even closer—here are a nose and two eyes in the head. Look still closer, and you will see the hint of a smile about the chipped edges of the lips.

It is a Maitreya bodhisattva, the work of some nameless country stonemason. Out of the many Buddhas which grace Buddhism, how is it that the Korean people have chosen the Maitreya to cherish and revere so? She is such an intimate part of our lives that we have come up with an affectionately familiar name for this Goddess of Mercy: in English it might come out something like Miss Mercy.

This Maitreya is a bodhisattva, not a Buddha, because she chose not to go to Nirvana but to return to the world and help others get to Nirvana. Sakyamuni told her that she would eventually attain Nirvana, but that would happen over five and a half billion years after his death, after she came back and helped all living creatures here to enlightenment.

Those who believe and live only in the present do not believe in the Maitreya.

Those, too, who see themselves as already among the elect, already "saved," who cannot feel the pain of unhappy, alienated living creatures, have nothing to do with her.

The fact that we have lived with such devotion to the Maitreya means that we have lived with a future of five billion years or so in our hearts. (Thus in the Korean language, while we have the words for the day after tomorrow, and three days from now, we have to use Chinese characters for that word which designates tomorrow, a day closer to the present.)

The fact that we have lived with such devotion to the Maitreya means that we have always been able to admit to ourselves the fact that we are not yet saved.

The fact that we have lived with such devotion to the Maitreya is proof that we regard the process of achieving enlightenment and becoming Buddha as more important than already being one.

The fact that we have lived with such devotion to the Maitreya is because we share the humanism of the Maitreya, who put off the bliss of full enlightenment and Nirvana so that she could come back to save each and every living being.

There are few on earth who have walked so closely and lived in such intimacy with the Maitreya as the Korean people. If you look at her posture, unique among all the Buddhist deity, you will know why. A Buddhist deity is either seated, in a lotus or half-lotus position (if he has achieved full enlightenment), or standing (if he has not yet achieved enlightenment). But the Maitreya is half-seated, half-standing, as if she were resting on a stool. The seated position shows the still serenity associated with completion, and the standing position shows that stirring which we can sense in lack of completion. The Maitreya is neither a seated Buddha nor a standing bodhisattva. Or we can say, in a more positive sense, she is half standing and half seated. But now look again. In that intermediate position, already one foot rests on her other leg; this is one step closer to the completely seated position, in near fulfillment of Sakyamuni's prophecy of her future Buddhahood. Both the bodhisattva and the Buddha live in the Maitreya.

The Korean reflects this duality which we find in the Maitreya's status and position. The negative side to this duality is that element of irresolution we have in our nature. But the positive and creative side of this duality in us is the intellectual understanding and the spiritual devotion that went into our creation of the Maitreya's likeness (now in the National Museum), which has impressed the world with its beauty.

Our Maitreya is the Buddha before Nirvana, the crown princess who shares the pain of humans. She is, simply put, *our* Maitreya.

Sister's Wicker Basket
바구니
Bakuni

In the old days when sister went out she did not bring with her any Christian d'Or handbag or Yves St. Laurent purse. She brought her wicker basket, that bulky thing that looked like it might be carrying a big balloon. And inside that bag were no cosmetics for powdering her nose, no money either.

It was empty. The wicker basket is not used only for keeping things in, like cosmetics or a small purse. It is used primarily to gather things. In the spring it is filled with greens, in the summer with mulberry leaves, and in the autumn with the leftovers from reaping. With this along we dig up things, pick things, gather things from the ground...in fact, we could describe its general function as that of collecting. Inside that basket lives and breathes the history of that era long in the past, before we began to plow and sow, when the cave dweller wandered the earth gathering what he needed to survive.

The wicker basket is not, like the dresser or the big wardrobe deep inside the room, something which beckons inward. It suggests going out. It brings to mind the bird's nest, that launching pad for the bird's ascent into the heavens. Another of its features is that it is more often empty than not. It is full only on the way back. So it is usually as light as if it existed in a state free of gravity.

When it is empty the wicker bag is closest to its prototype, and at its most beautiful.

To the shy lass who knew nothing of the outside world the wicker basket served as a strong ship for her departure on a voyage across the seas of the vast unknown. And so to our sister this basket was not only a simple utensil to help in her labor, like the sickle or the hoe. With the wicker basket along, the field where she went to pick greens became a dance floor. And she gathered not only greens but also the spring gossamer and its fragrance. The act of filling the wicker basket was an act of love.

When she went out for mulberry leaves she brought back a basket filled with romance. "Go out for mulberry leaves, come back with a sweetheart..." Just like that old ditty sings, the wicker basket served in both work and play. It saw no contrast between the two, nor between work and love, but provided for the same kind of union we see in the hand's palm and its back. In terms of clothing we could describe it in terms of overalls and party dress. Or what if, seeing sister going out to the fields with wicker basket in hand, we were given a choice, to compare her with either the honey bee or the butterfly? We would say that she was more like the butterfly than the honey bee. Both the butterfly

and the bee collect nectar, but the bee makes its beeline directly from one flower to another, while the butterfly flits about in her circling lines of matchless beauty on her meandering way.

It is easy to understand why the danseuse in our folk dances brings the wicker basket on stage with her. There is not the least feeling of incongruity in this basket's participation in the dance. On the contrary, we feel the dance could not do without it.

These days, when daughter comes back home in the evening, her handbag is always practically empty. There may be a few subway tickets, and some bits of change from what she has squandered that evening Leftovers, like tired memories. But remember how our sister came back home, her wicker basket stuffed with fragrant greens, and secrets shared by all from time immemorial.

Pants for People
바지

Baji

If you want to really know what it is when they talk about the functionalism and rationalism of the West, all you have to do is put on a pair of their trousers.

These trousers are made to clutch at the waist without allowing even an inch of leeway. The closer their fit, the more highly regarded the tailor. It is not only trousers. Even in women's skirts, the length can vary, but the waist has to be a perfect fit.

It is no exaggeration to say that the technology which got us to the moon originated in this concept of exact measurement. So be it. To the Korean, though, in his baggy trousers with their bulky cotton padding, there is nothing more ridiculous than a close fit.

Man's waist was never meant to be measured. His waist is never the same size. It is full after a person has eaten and when he is in good health, and contracts when he has not eaten for a while, or when he is ill. No matter how accurate the measurement of what he wears, a human is not some architectural product made from concrete, but is always in flux. The attempt to measure the human body for a comfortable fit brings to mind the story about the river boatman who dropped his knife in the water and marked an X on the spot with his finger so he could find the knife when he came back that way

again. How can a living body be measured? This folly of trying to measure the ever-changing body with a tape measure comes straight from the rationalism and functionalism of the West. And because of such a mentality, when the body expands a bit the trousers' waist is unbearably confining, and when the body shrinks a bit, you spend all day pulling up your trousers.

Thus the Korean designed the uni-size trousers, where you just fold in or fold out as your waistline requires. The unique feature of Korean trousers is that they are the world's largest in the waist, and have nothing to do with measuring, so that anyone can wear one's own or anyone else's trousers, in any circumstance. All you have to do is loosen or tighten the waist strap to suit the situation. It is the same with the skirt our women wear. The Korean has gone beyond the West's rationalistic concept of exact measurement to give his products the flexibility to adopt to any situation.

The discomfort we suffer in western trousers is indeed a result of modern industrial society, which in turn was born of functionalism and rationalism.

The human being is supposed to come before the clothes he wears, just as the cart is supposed to come after the horse. Clothes were meant to be worn by people,

they were not meant to wear themselves. But look at the suit. Even when it is taken off, it retains its stiff form. That is why it must be hung on a hanger after it is taken off. Korean clothes are different. They take on the three-dimensional form of the human when they are being worn, then resume their two-dimensional form when taken off. And so we do not hang them, we fold them.

Korean clothes do not exist for and of themselves, and so do not hold on to their own form when not being worn. In the West, the human fits himself to his clothes, his clothes wear him. The result, of course, is the alienation we see so much in western society.

The adjustable waist of Korean clothes represents the culture's flexible attitude towards material goods, its only inflexible rule being that they serve the interest and attend to the comfort of the people using them.

Gourd of Bounty

박

Bak

Tears well in the eye when the thatch-roof house comes to mind. In the monsoon the centipede makes its round on that thatch roof, and the thatch rots dark brown, looking as if someone spilled soy sauce all over it.

The thatch roof tells of our poverty and that wistful plaint, called *han*, which the Korean harbors in his bosom.

One can perhaps understand something of the heart of our unfortunate former dictator Park Chung-hee, who put so much of himself into eliminating the thatch roof from our countryside. He himself was born and raised under a thatch roof, and lived the sorrows of that poverty which he somehow blamed on this roof. But then again, why he had to replace this roof, which our ancestors had lived under for centuries, with that corrugated slate roof and its screaming reds and blues... We can hear our grandparents turning in their graves.

To them, improving the roof did not require changing this roof for another. What they did was simply to plant the gourd vine up on the thatch. With the gourd up there among the sorrows of life and occasional resentment toward poverty, that roof became a garden of productive beauty.

I have not heard of any people other than Koreans who have ever used their roof for a vegetable patch. But I do not think anyone would think of denigrating this as something done only in the desperation of straightened circumstances. This roof half covered with vines beautifies and transforms the wattle and daub hovel into a quaint country cottage. Look on some summer night, the fireflies dancing and the gourd blossoms white as moon beams, and you will know what those inside that home are dreaming there beneath that sagging thatch roof. Not even stifling poverty could rob them of their dreams. They use the gourd blossom, which graces the night and then sleeps at the kiss of the morning dew, to embellish their poverty. And so, because the gourd provides both pleasure and bounty, the thatch roof can do the same.

The gourd is blessed with a paradox. Other fruits and vegetables are worth no more than what you can eat of them. With the gourd, though, after you have scraped out all its meat and are left with the shell, it begins its second life. Now its ruling principle is not substance, but emptiness. What was there matters less than what is not there. This is what accomplishes its primary purpose. And maybe it is this paradox which allows it to serve many purposes rather than stubbornly stick to one specialized task. This multi-purpose instrument can scoop up water for you from the spring, help you measure out rice from the rice chest; a small one can serve as a table-top container for soy sauce, a bigger one can serve as a canister for rice cakes. And when you are relaxing with friends, use it to scoop up the rice wine out of the barrel or to wear as a mask in some silly dance. Then, when it gets cracked and you cannot use it in the house anymore, use it out in the field for spreading fertilizer. It never stops working.

No form of poverty is severe enough to beat the power of the gourd. When the poverty grinds hard enough, a Korean will look up at the gourd growing there on that thatch roof, and remember the tale of Hungbu. He was the impoverished but honest and generous younger brother who was deprived by his elder brother of the inheritance bequeathed both of them by their father, but in the end blessed, for his goodness, with magic gourds carrying a bounty of treasures. Koreans dream of that day–someday–when, if they are as good and kind as Hungbu, they can split open their very own magic gourd and live a life free of want.

There is the gourd vine up on that thatch roof. How could anyone fail to see that and instead dwell only on the anguish of poverty?

The Boot Sock
버선
Boson

They tell the story of how when one company offered one free pair of stockings in every package of their instant soup, sales plummeted. The consumers had subconsciously tasted someone's foot in their soup.

Of all the parts of the human body, the foot is the sorriest. The foot is that part which comes in direct contact with the ground, which makes it the dirtiest and the most abused part of the body. Those five wiggling appendages (the most revolting being that withered baby toe) and that knob on the side which juts out like some tumor...the foot is so ridiculous it defies description. And so genteel women in the medieval age hid the silly things under those skirts which hung all the way to the floor.

The Korean, however, turned this unfortunate part of the body into a thing of beauty. He used his refined sense of design to give us the boot sock.

The western stocking assumes concrete form only when put on the foot. The particular form which it takes is that of the foot wearing it. No matter how good they may be in the West at designing clothes, they have not yet been able to figure out how to do something for the foot. Every other piece of western clothing, except for that pitiful stocking, has its own identity, its own form independent of the body wearing it. The

stocking, though—when you take that thing off it just lays there limp, as creepy as the dead skin a snake has just slithered out of. The Japanese *tabi*, much like the boot sock, is made to fit the form of the feet exactly, and when it is taken off it looks as if someone's chopped-off foot is laying there—hideously realistic.

And then there is the Korean boot sock. It beautifies the foot by providing distinctive form. All the graceful lines of the boot sock sweep together to meet in a hooked peak at the toe, something every bit as beautiful as the hip on the roof corners on a Korean temple. No, no need to worry about that protruding big toe showing. The boot sock is a deviation from anatomical engineering in that no part of it too closely resembles its corresponding part on the foot.

When you take off the boot sock it retains its attractive form. It is originally for the foot, yes, but also a good decorative piece for the room.

The boot sock's lack of direct resemblance to the foot has given rise to some humorous incidents. It sometimes seems difficult for the uninitiated foreigner to know that it is supposed to go on the foot. There is that anecdote (whether true or not) about when, during Japan's Edo period, a pair of boot socks were presented to a distinguished

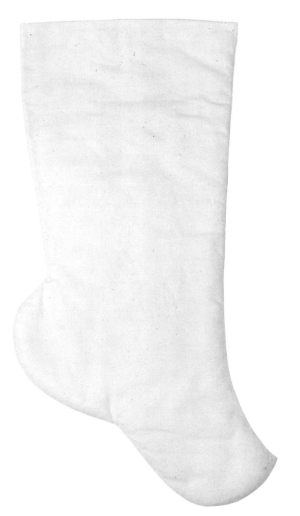

personage of Japan, they were mistaken for and used as headgear. Thus the boot sock was jokingly referred to as the "Edo cap." Westerners might enhance this anecdote: the "Edo stocking cap."

As I have mentioned elsewhere in these pages, Koreans, who like roominess and flexibility in everything they wear, and do not like something which fits exactly without even that inch or so of leeway, make an exception with the boot sock. It is not loose and roomy like our skirts and trousers, it is a snug fit. The boot sock does not come off easily once it is on. Any Korean will remember that experience of greeting mother on her return home, and trying to help pull her boot socks off, only to end up *thump!* on the rump.

We can say that the boot sock is the embodiment of the Korean aesthetic. Unlike in the West, the foot appears often in Korean literature and song, and that description of the heroine Chunhyang stepping so delicately in her boot socks suggests to one the ultimate in beauty. Real beauty is not an enhancement of something that we already think is beautiful. Real beauty is the successful transfiguration of something that is unpleasant to look at into something that pleases the eye.

The Korean boot sock could never be thought of in terms of that stocking which ruined the company that offered it in a package of soup.

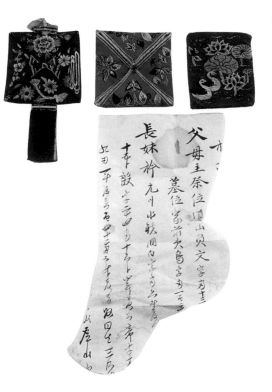

Dreamy Pillow Ends

베갯모

Bekaetmo

Freud said that dreams come from suppressed sexuality in the subconscious. And he devoted his life to analyzing such dreams.

Koreans of long ago, however, especially their simple women, believed that dreams come from the pillow. And to bring that dream alive they devoted their lives to embroidering beautiful things at the circular ends of their cylindrical pillows. In one classic text from hundreds of years ago is a description of such a pillow: "The sack is of bleached ramie, stuffed with aromatic plants, and both ends are embroidered with the most exquisite swirls of red silk gauze—a lovely lotus blossom." One can easily picture how beautiful that pillow must have been.

Because the pillow is for resting one's head in sleep, it is not all that big in proportion to the human body. So you have to fit the design of the pillow end into a pretty small space. Also, because the pillow end stays in the bedroom it is rather reclusive. It is not like silk clothing or other formal attire for going out and meeting others. It is found in that secret and dark place, where two in closest intimacy share one spot. We cannot say there is no relationship here with Freud's talk of the sexuality of dreams, but the sexuality related to the pillow end is not some twisted, suppressed, depressing thing.

It is something exquisite and fertile.

On some pillow ends are embroidered a pair of parent phoenix with their seven chicks, with the intent of yet another go at their fertile act of procreation, and on another you might see a bat in the form of the Chinese character for good fortune.

Yes, even something as dignified, profound and stolid as Chinese characters appears in this small universe of the pillow end. Here, though, the characters are no longer in black but of colors which bloom like a bouquet of blossoms and spring leaves, changing those solemn characters into resplendently auspicious signs promising such gifts as wealth and many male offspring.

We see the nature of the pillow end not only in symbols promising many sons, many children, abundance, but also in representations of Taoist immortals, in the bamboo and the roe, and in those Ten Immortals: sun, moon and cloud, mountain, brook and lake, deer, crane and turtle, pine and herb of perennial youth. Images of these Ten Immortals can appear on almost any household item, but nowhere do they appear as full of life as they do on the pillow end. Here is no sense of reality to restrict them, and they appear as part of a dream.

Rest your head back on this pillow now, and enjoy a view of a congenial gathering of the Ten Immortals. The red sun and moon both hover there above that stylized cloud, and under this roams the deer tasting of the herb of perennial youth at the base of the pine, whose age-twisted trunk reflects the abstract swirls on the back of the turtle, which is too busy growing old to notice the crane riding on aromatic wind. All these characters are here together to make a dream which has been dreamed by our ancestors for hundreds of years.

Not one of the characters in this embroidery on the pillow end is by itself. Each one has a partner. Like the mandarin duck pillow, which is actually a pair of pillows signifying connubial bliss, this is a world of affection and union. In the small space of pillow ends is the dream of all people being joined together as a family, and all things in the universe becoming one, loving all.

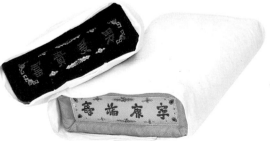

The Lives of a Folding Screen
병풍
Byongpung

Western culture, which capitalizes the first person singular "I," has its basis in the wall, which separates you and I. This culture is depicted succinctly in the myth of Oedipus, when the Sphinx asks Oedipus, "Who are you?" and Oedipus responds, "You know who I am." That problem of the disparate you and I has always existed in the West. And in this way the "me-first culture" maintains itself by building walls to separate its rooms, and walls again to separate its cities.

The epitome of the wall is the isolating basement room. In the West the concept of privacy is the utmost consideration, its basic system of punishment (by sequestering in prisons), and is a basic element in its poetry and philosophy—all these originate in the thick basement wall. Where did Dostoevsky's words come from but the damp walls of a basement cell? And you can hear the cry of the basement's black cat in Poe's lucid intellect.

In a residence in Korea there was no such thing as a basement. And the ideal wall for the Korean has no relation with any basement. The Korean concept of the wall expresses itself best in the folding screen. When the literati of Korea wanted to establish an inner space for the act of creation, for instance, they did it simply by setting up a folding screen.

Of all the walls mankind has produced the lightest and most flexible is the folding screen. If one wants to move a western wall he has to dig down to the foundation, but to move a folding screen all one has to do, obviously, is fold it up.

Fold up six or twelve panels, and they become one. Open up the screen and it

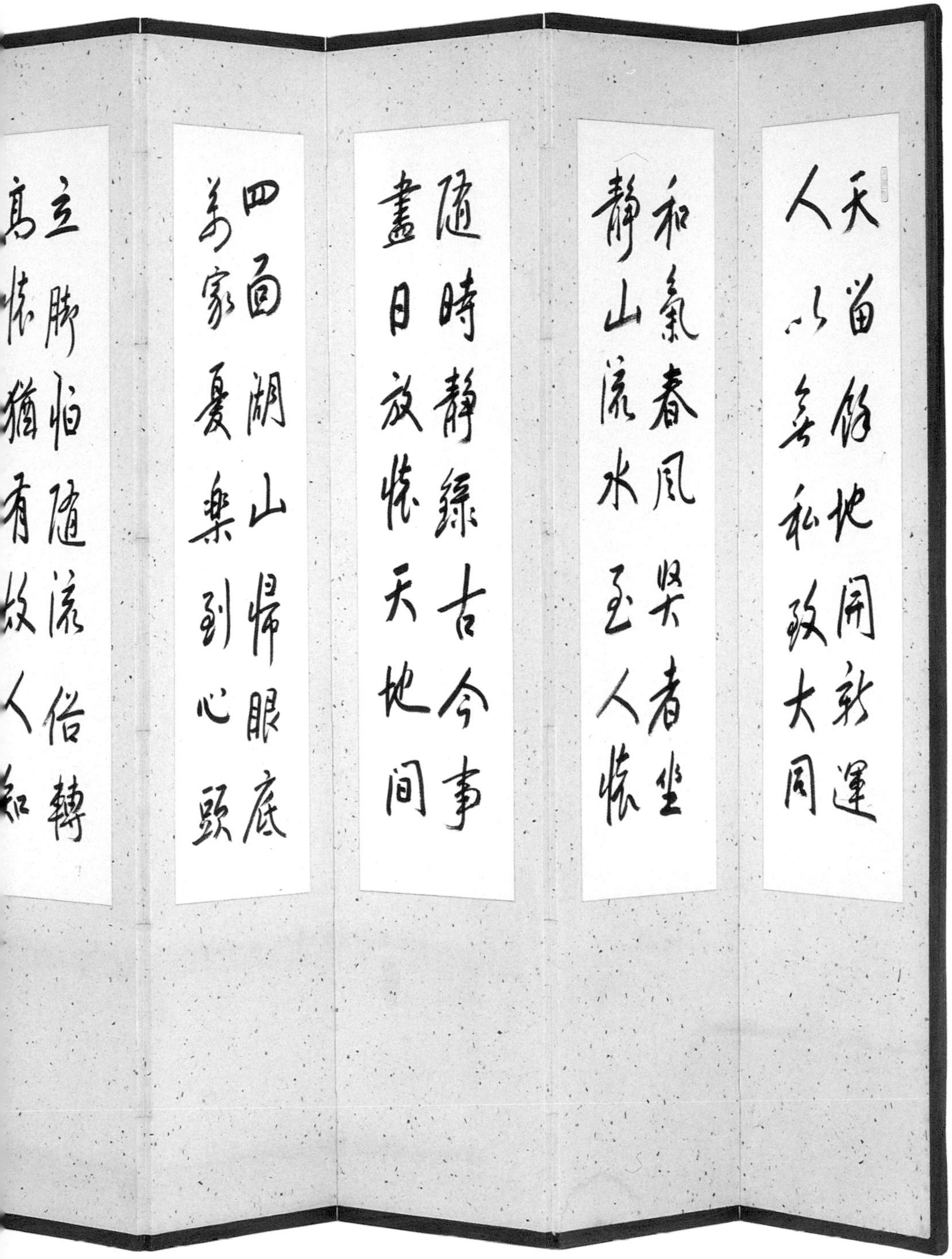

和氣春風吳者坐　靜山流水玉人悵

人以善私致大同　天道當地開新運

立腳怕隨流俗轉　高懷猶有故人知

四面湖山歸眼底　萬家憂樂到心頭

盡日放悵天地間　隨時靜綠古今事

becomes a wall. Fold it and you have rid yourself of one wall.

Set up my flower-and-bird screen and I am just married. With my books-and-brushes screen I am a scholar. And with my mountains-and-stream screen I become a Taoist immortal, idling away the day like a retired scholar in my rustic retreat. In ten folding screens are ten expressions of myself. With ten folding screens I am in ten different places.

Westerners have always tried to beautify their walls; the decoration of walls is inherent in the development of their art. One difference between East and West is that the East's folding screen is not a wall with a work of art hung on it, but a work of art in itself. And too, in this one work there are several different compositions, depending on how many panels and which of them one chooses to open. So much different from one simple stationary painting on a wall. This portable wall of the East is a portable work of art. And when you have done with it and want to view another, just fold it up and it disappears.

Just as one folding screen sets the stage for the play of newlyweds, another establishes the boundary which separates the living from the dead at a wake. Shakespeare illustrated a human's life in terms of the diaper and the shroud, but in Korea life begins and ends with the folding screen. A Korean's life comes and goes like the opening and folding of a screen. Just like "you" and "I" become "we" when the screen which separates us for a while is taken up and put away.

All-Purpose Wrapper
보자기
Bojagi

Capitalism is based on the human proclivity to store possessions. Crates, lockers, chests and storerooms are the offspring of capitalism. The more one owns, the bigger his crates. What in fact is a house if not just a very big crate?

Capitalism began to develop seriously not from our desire to accumulate, but when we got the idea to move our possessions, in order to barter them, with a portable crate. The introduction of trade brought the suitcase to the West, and the *bojagi* to Korea and Asia.

Bojagi? It is just a big, square, simple piece of cloth. You close it by tying its four corners over its load. That is all there is to it.

There is a basic difference between the suitcase and the bojagi, not to be found, though, in any simplistic distinction of primitive as opposed to civilized. Look closely at these two devices, and you can see the same basic functional concept. The suitcase has one additional, extraneous function, of course: onto the basic form of a crate a handle has been attached. Its solid form of a crate means that it is always the same size and shape, whether chock full or empty. A suitcase stubbornly insists on forever being a suitcase, and could care less whether it is doing its job carrying something or not. How arrogant.

The bojagi, on the other hand, expands and contracts with the amount it is carrying, and gets its form from the nature of its contents. At times you will see it bulging with things like those dried pollack with their heads sticking out, and then again it can be as flat as an envelope when some letters or documents are all there is to carry. And when it has nothing to carry, its three dimensions deflate into the flatness of two dimensions, for all practical purposes relinquishing its own existence. In contrast to the suitcase, the bojagi adapts itself to what is and what is not inside.

Look at how the suitcase and the bojagi are used. There is only one term to describe what we can do with a suitcase: load. But for the bojagi there are several verbs to describe its several functions: wrap (*ssa-da*), wear over the head (*ssu-da*), put it over someone else's head (*ssuiu-da*), wrap around oneself (*turu-da*), cover (*top-da*), hide something (*kari-da*), and countless others. If you were a thief, you would not need to both wear a mask and carry a suitcase if you had a bojagi. Put it over your face and it is a mask, and after you make your hit, use it as a suitcase.

Imagine a car being able to change its form and size according to how many passengers were using it. It could, if only it had the flexibility and multi-purpose qualities of the freely expanding and contracting bojagi. That car would really be something: several square meters at your service when you are riding, and then when you get out it practically disappears.

But why only a car? Any device or equipment with the accommodating philosophy of the bojagi could help make our culture a little more pleasant, a little more aescetically pleasing–a little more for the human.

A Fan for Winter

부채

Buchae

Koreans love the hand fan. In a classic from the Koryo dynasty (918-1392 A.D.) we find, "Koryo people carry the hand fan around with them even in the middle of winter." Even way back then they could not be without their hand fan. But it was not because they were especially susceptible to heat—its utility was not its most important feature.

There is another expression from the classics, "Charcoal brazier in the summer, fan in the winter." This means that, if evaluated purely from the point of utility, there exists nothing more useless than a brazier in the summer or that fan in the winter. None of our utensils, though, exists only for its utility. Even the sword and the shield, which lose their practical usefulness when the war has been won or lost, serve an additional function as ornamentation for the wall. Was that not true of the heavily ornamented shield of Achilles in Homer's Iliad?

The fan in the summer, when we are not using it to fan ourselves, has as much practical value as the fan in the winter. But the fan in both summer and winter has aesthetic value. And so it transcends the seasons, because it can find its justification for existence in itself, not only in its utility. The folding fan, which we fold when we do not need it and open up when we do, is the ideal form of human tool, in which both function and ornamentation coexist exquisitely. The hand fan has that broad surface which provides the perfect setting for some of our best classical art. This decorated hand fan is on occasion used as a kind of veil, to hide the

face, as we can see in many folk paintings of the master Tanwon. It is also an essential element in several classic dances and shamanistic dances.

While it is true of all handicrafts that aesthetics are of even more importance than utility, this is still truer of the *hapjuk* folding fan, with spokes made of double slips of bamboo. This is evident in the way it is crafted. It has been said that "the double-ribbed fan begins with the selection of the bamboo grove." If the grove gets too much water or if it is too close to a house the bamboo's tone will be off, rendering this bamboo useless as far as the hand fan is concerned; and when the bamboo is cut, great care must be taken not to nick it because this would destroy its color. Even the season in which it is cut is of critical importance. If not during the lunar month of July (usually more than a month later than the solar July), it will have to be done between the end of lunar September and the February of the following year. In other months there are problems such as insects. So these are the only periods which can ensure the finest quality bamboo.

With something made so carefully and with such devotion and skill, even if it were to lose its function its form and color alone would justify its existence.

In this electronic age, when we use the electric fan and the air conditioner instead of the hand fan, what happens when they go out of order, or when the season changes? They become as useless as rubbish.

Old pottery, even when it is not being used in accordance with its original function, increases in value and becomes prized as an antique, not only because of its historical value, but more because of its form and lustre. Just like a hand fan in the winter is still a fan.

A Most Communicative Brush

붓

But

Meaning is conveyed through signs. Look at those tracks in the sand on the seashore, and you can read the small dramas of the aquatic bird and the crab who hides under the sand. The words produced by humans are only one kind among the many scattered around the shores of life.

A sign is an impression which is set down to convey meaning, and it was originally scratched with something sharp and hard enough to impress it upon a surface. This is why one linguist claims that we get the Korean noun for writing (*kul*) from the verb scratch (*kulk-da*). In Japanese, the sounds of the words for write (ka-kku) and scratch (*hi-kka-kku*) are similar. Even in English the word for writing means scratch.

Like the tiger staking out his territory uses his claws to scratch his mark at the base of a tree, the human's first instrument for illustrating a notion must have been his finger nail. After that he would have used something like a bone or the branch of a tree, and later, to preserve what he wrote for a long time, he used a sharp metal object to etch it in stone or clay tablets. So scratch became etch, and setting down meaning through signs developed into etching it in words.

With the discovery of paper, etching evolved into writing. In view of such a history, we can see proof in the metal pen of the West that, although the West has entered the era of paper, its writing instruments have yet to emerge from the era of scratching and etching.

What happens to the paper when you press hard on the western fountain pen or ballpoint pen? It tears. The pen is not writing, it is scratching. Thus, although we can see a message, we cannot see any trace of the person who wrote it. This is because the writing produced by a pen is the trace of the writing instrument, not the writer.

But with the writing brush, no matter how hard you press you cannot tear the paper. The brush is not an extension of the finger-nail. Because the brush is soft it gathers and passes on strength. This allows it to convey the delicate and profound rhythm of the writer's spirit. It conducts the spirit of the writer with the trueness and facility of an electric current, whereas the pen conducts not much more than its own scratching.

The hand which holds this soft brush is moved by the shoulder, and the shoulder gets its strength from the breast, which is in turn powered by the muscles of the stomach. But it all starts in the toes, which must be planted firmly to the ground. A master artist once wrote, in his treatise "On Calligraphy," that writing comes from the feet, which means of course that writing can be produced only by calling up that primal energy which resides in the earth. True writing, then, more than being an expression of meaning, is an impression of the spirit itself.

The Japanese developed their culture around the finely honed sword; the Koreans developed their culture around the softest of brushes. One of these brushes was the "weasel tail brush" which the Chinese envied so.

Paper is not something to be scratched, carved in, or etched on. It is to be written on. The reason there is no calligraphy in the West is because theirs is not a culture in which writing is intended to leave the impression of the writer's essential spirit. Thus the culture of the ball point pen is changing directly into a culture of typewriter and word processor. There is no greater contrast than that between the mindless mechanical writer and the weal tail writing brush, which shows the original spirit of the writer.

Crossbar in a Hairpin

비녀

Binyo

The beauty of the female might well be explained by the fact that this beauty can take so many forms, ranging from the fecund fullness of the housewife to the sterile slimness of the harlot. One form of beauty promises regeneration, the other unburdened pleasure.

The typical female in folk art was round and full, and even when she was a harlot, her beauty was drawn in imitation of that beauty associated with the housewife. In modern times, though, it is the reverse. Now the housewife wants to emulate the thin-waisted, barren beauty of the harlot.

Not more than ten years ago a woman who painted her nails and face was signalling that she worked as a woman of the night. These days, that same signal is sent in the way housewives dress. Many explain this as the result of the degeneration of morals in

modern society. More important than this, though, is the transformation in the way we regard fertility today. For over five billion generations of human existence fertility was one of the most highly valued of woman's attributes; it is now often considered as bordering on the criminal. As a result, to housewife or harlot, sex is seldom any longer the means to procreation but an end in itself. In terms of sexuality the housewife and harlot share a common role.

And so the Korean woman's chignon and that long, graceful hairpin she wore with it now and forever serve no more use than does some dimly remembered myth from the distant past. An integral part of that past was the long hairpin. The basic function of the hairpin was to keep the hair pulled back tightly in a bun, like a chignon. It was used not to make the hair alluring but to keep it

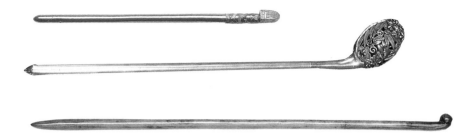

in its proper place. Even the most expensive jade or coral pin was not basically different from the wooden pin; all these pins manifested a spirit of strict propriety. Korean women began to wear this pin during the reign of King Yongjo, in the seventeenth century, with his mandate that all of them would wear their hair in a chignon as one way of eliminating extravagance in dress and behavior.

The problem was not only material extravagance. The pin sticks through the tightly bound knot of hair crosswise, and one end has a hook to prevent the pin from slipping out. The pin was the crossbar on the door to the woman, to help her preserve her womanly virtues and protect her chastity. To translate its figurative meaning into western terms, it is what the key was to the chastity belt of the Middle Ages.

How a woman wears her hair shows what kind of woman she is. There is a significant element of contrast between free-flowing hair and the hair which this pin held in place. In the movie industry in Korea all the director has to do to give a movie a risque reputation is to have his actress pull out that hairpin and let her tresses fall free.

And so, achieving intimacy with the modern woman, who uses no hairpin, is as easy as getting into a house with no crossbar, the door left wide open. Which makes getting in all that much of a bore.

When one sees how the beauty of the harlot has all but taken over the bedroom these days, what frequently comes to mind is that slim, straight, strong and beguiling crossbar hairpin.

The Farmers' Band
사물놀이
Samulnori

Korea, like any other culture, has various forms of classical and popular traditional music. One of its most distinctive forms is the music performed by its farmers.

This "farmers' music" is based on four percussion instruments. One is very much like the western cymbal, giving off a high, sharp sound, but struck by a stick rather than another cymbal. There is also the mellower gong, bigger than the cymbal. The other two instruments are drums, each with two heads. The larger one has the general shape of the hourglass, and the other is squat. When you hear the music produced by these four instruments you will probably find your shoulders swinging in spite of yourself, in time to an exhilarating rhythm coursing through you.

Though the feeling produced by these instruments is difficult to explain in scientific terms, we can begin to understand if we analyze the symbolism inherent in them. First, let us consider their number. Things in nature often come in four. There are the four points of the compass, the four seasons... If we analyze their correspondence to each other we can get a feeling for the bond which exists among the four percussion instruments.

Eastern philosophy suggests basic polar relationships between north and south and summer and winter. Dominated by these polar elements are the other directions and seasons. West is primarily dominated by north, and east is dominated by south, as autumn is in winter's realm and spring is in summer's. At the same time, there is correspondence between directions and seasons not in each other's realm. Autumn, for example, while it leads to winter, comes from summer. So these dominated elements allow for a smooth cyclical progression between the dominant primary poles, between north and south and winter and summer.

The system of the music produced by our four percussion instruments is identical to this schemata of nature, which was established thousands of years ago to help us understand how the universe and all of life work. Music's system, of course, is based on sound. Two of our four percussion instruments have metallic sounds, and two have the sound which comes from striking tautly stretched animal hide. So in our farmers music, too, we have a relationship of basic characteristics, of organic and inorganic. From the two drums comes the sound which organic hide will produce, and the cymbal and gong produce the sound of inorganic brass. The sound of the drum is mellow and deep, a thick, rich resonance, whereas the cymbal and the gong give off a high, sharp sound. The two drums get you in the pit of

the stomach, and the cymbal and gong go for the ear.

So we see that music, too, is ultimately based on two poles, just like nature. Now, if we consider all four of our metallic and hide instruments the same as we previously did nature's four directions and seasons, we will come up with the very same cycle. The gong and the hourglass drum are thought of as being the dominant poles. Just as the poles of spring and autumn and east and west, while essential elements in nature's cycle, are subordinate to their dominant poles, there is yet correspondence with another pole. In farmers' music the cymbal is in the realm of the gong. But the gong sound, because of the gong's substantial size, is not as striking as the cymbal and, even though its sound is of metal, there is something in it which resembles the sound of the drum. The hourglass drum has a sharper and clearer sound than the squat drum, so that, while its sound is produced by hide, it also relates to the metal cymbal. So these instruments correspond even in opposition. The gong could be regarded as a drum producing an organic sound, and the hourglass drum a cymbal producing an inorganic sound.

East and west, as we know, in their positions between north and south, provide for a continuous spatial cycle, as do spring and

autumn a continuous chronological cycle. These elements are basic to the operation of everything in the universe, including our instruments for music. The folk music which uses our percussion instruments is an agent of nature, and puts into our soul these four elemental forces which turn opposing poles into complementary elements of an inclusive cycle.

Once in us the rhythm holding the cycle of these four forces fuses these forces into yin and yang, the absolutely ultimate forces which govern the universe as a whole and dwell in every individual substance in the universe, including the directions, seasons and music. Then these two poles cleave apart into the primary elements of wood and fire, metal and water. At this point, that percussion rhythm still lingering within the human, nature's synthesizer, inspires the human to incorporate these elements into himself. Thus it is that each of us is a composite of all the elemental forces in life.

And so we see why this farmers' music means so much to the Korean. That exaltation we feel in the music produced by these instruments is, after all, none other than an experience of the primal forces of the universe in creative interaction.

Ethics of the Floor Table
상
Sang

China, Korea and Japan cohabit the same Far East Asia cultural sphere. While Koreans and Japanese dine on the floor at the low table, however, the Chinese sit on a chair, at the same kind of table used in the West.

A sixteenth-century Christian missionary wrote in comparing Japanese and western cultures that, whereas the dining table of the West occupies one place before, during and after meals, the Japanese set their table in the kitchen and carry it out to where the meal is going to be eaten. This points to one major difference between the two dining tables.

The western dining table is there in the dining room or kitchen whether anyone is dining or not, and exists there of itself. The Korean dining table, though, appears only when it is time to eat, and disappears with the dirty dishes after the meal. In this way the Korean table is like Korean bedding. Just as any room in a Korean house becomes a bedroom when the quilt and mat are spread, any of those rooms will become a dining room when the low table is set up there. Thus, once in place, the Korean table determines the nature of the place.

This dining table differs from its western counterpart in yet another way. The way the Korean table is used distinguishes the role

and rank of each person who sits at it. If one uses the table by himself, before the others in the family, he is the master of the house. Those who eat next and share the table are on a roughly equal level. And those who use that same table after it has been moved from the "dining room" into the kitchen are the women and servants, the lowest in rank.

One might say that when all in the family eat at the same table together this is democracy in action, and that when all eat at different times and in different configurations, here is a hierarchical feudal society. Certainly, while eating at feudalism's table one learns both the ethics and principles of that society. But what exactly are these ethics and principles? A closer look will enlighten us of the fact that among them are those principles of equality and freedom which democracy touts as its own exclusive creations.

Those feudal ethics which are instilled in us at the Korean dining table are only superficially different from the ethics of democracy. One of these ethics is equality. Those at or near the top of the household's hierarchy must honor this ethic by leaving enough food for those who are going to eat at that table next. In terms of democracy, call this equality; in terms of feudalistic society,

call it self-abnegation. Another example of this is one of the rules in the table manners of genteel society in Korea. Once the diner's chopsticks have cleaned off one side of the fish, he does not turn over the fish to get more. That other side of the fish is reserved for those who will follow at that table. So, at the Korean table, if those dining together do not cooperate and share with each other, they cannot eat. This is how at the Korean dining table we get special training in self-restraint and yielding to others, what democratic society calls equality.

Next, let us turn to the principle of freedom. A western meal, with its appetizers, main course and dessert, is as tightly structured an activity as writing a thesis, with its introduction, body and conclusion. Is this the democratic concept of freedom? At a Korean meal everything that is going to be eaten is right there in the center of the table, for everyone to eat in his own way. Because of this freedom of choice there is more liberty at the Korean table than at any other. With all those hands and chopsticks darting back and forth over that splendid array of side dishes, trying to predict what you will end up with is like trying to predict what number the ball in the roulette wheel is going to end up on. But the diner is, nevertheless, as free as the butterfly making its rounds from flower to flower.

In the West they do, indeed, eat together at the same democratic table. But at this table one does not eat directly from those dishes in the center of the table, as is done on the Korean table. Everyone is, for all practical purposes, eating alone, because basically each has on his own plate all the food he is going to get.

With the Korean table's distinctive nature of having no set course and allowing everyone to eat what he wants and how he wants, more important than the taste of the food is that the table legs creak at the abundance of the many foods on top. The reason for this abundance is to ensure that, after everyone is finished eating what and as he pleases, there is still some left over for those following. The philosophy of the Korean floor table is to put the principles of equality and individual freedom into real practice.

The Porch's Beams and Rafters

서까래

Sokkarae

Korea's planked porch, the *maru*, is an intermediate space which connects inside and outside. We can not get into the house from outside, or to the outside from in the house, without passing through the maru, which is half inside and half outside. So the light here is also a filtered blend of both inside and outside.

The architecture of this porch also has a character intermediate between interior and exterior. The feature of outside space is freedom and complete exposure. It is decorated with nature's earth, rocks and trees. The design and structural features of the interior, on the other hand, are covered by processed materials like paper and fabric. We paper our ceilings, and even use a strong varnished paper to cover the floor. Posts inside are also covered with paper and therefore practically invisible.

The porch, however, is half exposed and half concealed. This space sets up the boundary between nature and civilization. If you pull up the hanging doors of the maru, you are outside. That is why the bamboo blind looks so good when you decide to hang it there for the summer in place of the heavy doors, to keep the house cool. You do not find in the maru either of the two extremes of floor paper or earth, because the maru's floor is made from thick wood planks, a felicitous compromise. On

the maru the posts show themselves but, while you can recognize the post as part of a tree, it has been sanded and varnished, so that even this post comprises a dual nature.

The main beam in the roof over the maru, in its important role of establishing the maru's design, is exposed, and its thickness indicates the size and status of the whole house. Its appearance makes it seem as if a whole tree were cut down in the forest and placed there, but it is nothing like the raw logs of the western log cabin, which keep their bark. In this main beam nature survives intact, but at the same time we see here the presence of the human. So here we do not have the fresh taste of freshly harvested produce, but the processed taste of kimch'i, our fermented and spiced cabbage. The wood outside the house is that of the living tree of the fields, while the main beam is the very same living tree, only enhanced by the hand of the carpenter.

The tree inside the house has been turned into something that, for all anyone can tell, might as well be a metal or cement post, because it is completely covered with paper. Here we have a process of tree becoming lumber becoming paper; we see something of this in the division of architectural space of the entire household, from yard to maru to interior.

The rafter manifests the maru's distinctive

feature of intermediate space. The structure of the maru ceiling is not hidden by paper, as the ceiling is inside the house. Its full nature is exposed, and you can see the form and color of the rafters which support the roof. In these rafters you can imagine the ribs of tile on the roof outside climbing up toward the roof's ridge line and then the sky; or through those rafters you can follow the roof's rib lines down to their eaves and off to the ridges of the mountains in the distance.

In becoming a rafter the log's original appearance is slightly altered, and so the rafter is the borderline between nature and civilization. While it has the flowing lines of nature it also has the geometric lines of civilization. This is where it gets its particular beauty. The different rafters in one ceiling, whether they are parallel, in a horseshoe, or fan out, all have been drawn with one design in mind and combine in one geometric pattern. But each individual rafter at the same time displays those varying lines of nature which we find in the living tree.

So when we lie on the maru and gaze up at those rafters we can feel that special ambience which cannot be felt either inside the house or out in the yard. Those rafters endow empty space with a frame. In this we can see the Korean structuring the sky.

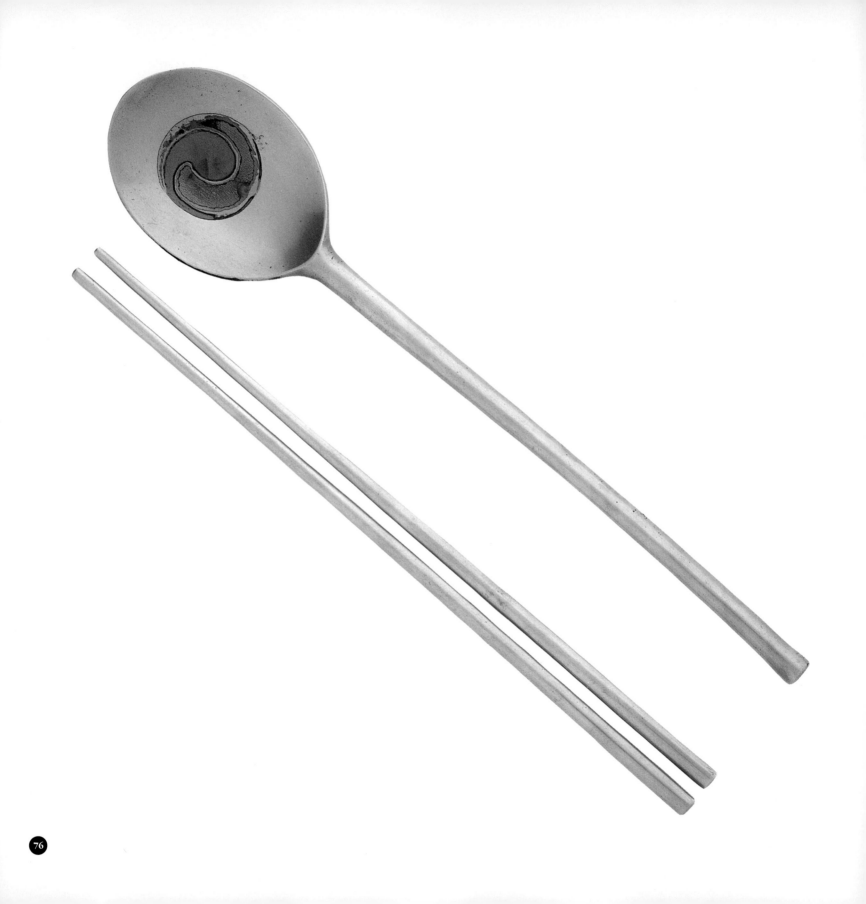

The Yin-Yang Union of Spoon and Chopsticks
수저

Sujo

The chopstick identifies one culture common to China, Korea and Japan. Historical research by anthropologists tell us that way back in time the chopstick in all three of these countries was commonly made of wood, so that it is difficult to determine exactly where the chopstick originated. However, as bronze chopsticks have been excavated from sites dating back to Yin China, it would seem that the Chinese were the first to use them.

In one Chinese classic it is reported that the Japanese ate with their hands, which would suggest that Japanese civilization was later in developing. It is therefore logical to consider Korea as having been at an intermediate stage of development between the Japanese and Chinese.

Why is it that we find several nations in the East Asian cultural sphere using chopsticks and Westerners using the fork and knife? There are several explanations for this, but we do know that one good reason is the fact that western food is served in large pieces, and the food eaten with chopsticks is served already cut in small pieces. If steak were served already diced in small morsels, they would not need the knife at the dining table.

That young girl with her large scissors is a standard feature of the Korean ribs restau-rant. She is there to cut the meat for the customers while it is cooking. (The uniniti-ated happening upon this girl might wonder if he got the wrong directions and ended up in a tailor shop.) If she were not there to cut the meat for us, though, it would be every-one for himself, and one would have no choice but to arm himself with knife and fork, like going out to the field of battle or dining at a western table.

The western way of eating is "Self service." Western food is not pre-seasoned. The individual seasons his food himself. No wonder individualism originated in the West, where one person prepares the food and the other eats it.

It is said that the spirit of motherhood is lacking in Western food. Most humans have their first meals cuddled at their mother's breast. The basic principle in food is this mother-child interaction, that of serving and being served. This principle is inherent in the chopstick, which is designed not to allow us to cut food ourselves but to eat food which someone else has cut for us. And in the chopstick resides another principle of eating, that of parallel interaction. The two chopsticks are always used in pairs, and through this show a you-and-I interdependency. One chopstick by itself can pick up nothing. The spirit of a pair of chopsticks is the spirit of two mates, and only with its mate does the chopstick fully realize its nature.

A higher form of this companion spirit is Korea's combination of spoon and chopsticks. In China and Japan they do indeed often use the spoon along with the chopsticks, but it is only in Korea where that the spoon is always found on the table right there with the chopsticks. The Korean meal is based on a balance and harmony of liquids and solids; just as light and dark combine in all material things, the Korean meal consists of a yin-yang correspondence of liquid and solid. This is true neither of the salad in the West nor of the pickled radish side dish in Japan. And so the Korean must always have both spoon and chopsticks there on the table. Our chopsticks handle the yang-natured solids, and the spoon takes care of the yin-natured liquids. The physical form, too, of each mate in this pair embodies the yin-yang principle, in that the chopstick, the yang element, is long and pointed, and the spoon, the yin element, is concave.

The chopsticks and spoon are a union of male and female, mother and child, solid and liquid. In this pair of chopsticks and spoon we see the warm communication between the giver of food and its receiver.

The Old Straw Shoe

신발

Shinbal

The Shoe has a more intimate relationship with the person wearing it than does any other piece of clothing. Just analyze a few Korean words related to clothes, and you will agree. In *shinbal*, the word for shoe, *shin* means shoe and *bal* means foot. You see how the word itself establishes an inseparable relationship between the shoe and its foot. And in the word *maenbal*, which means shoeless, *maen* means bare, and again *bal* means foot. So the one word again includes shoe—this time its absence—and foot. The verb which denotes the act of putting the shoe on the foot is *shin-da*, *shin* again being the word for shoe (with-*da* indicating that it is a verb).

Other clothes do not have such an intimate relationship with the person wearing them. We *kki-da* (slip on) a *changkap* (glove), *ssu-da* (put on the head) a *moja* (hat), and *ip-da* (put on) a pair of *paji* (trousers). No obvious relation exists here between the forms of the object nouns and the verbs which they are used with. So we see that, unlike other clothes, when we speak of the body and the shoes we can legitimately refer to them as mates.

We might look further. The shoes one wears are also an element in distinguishing identity. Cinderella's glass slippers distinguished her from all her competitors. And there is the ancient Korean legend from the *Heritage of Three Kingdoms*, a history written around six hundred years ago which tells of the ill-fated lovers Yonorang and Seonyo, who left their four shoes lined up next to each other on the shore of the ocean they walked into together, to let others know who went where and did what.

There are many cases in which the features of the shoe tell not only of the individual but also of the distinguishing elements of an entire culture. We say that being without shoes identifies the primitive, and having shoes identifies the civilized. And so in Korea among theatre people they have their own jargon for people in the audience who are visiting from the countryside. They call them "rubber slippers," that footgear resembling the form of the old straw shoes, which even city people used to wear until a few years ago but are worn now, and rarely at that, only in the countryside.

We sometimes refer derisively to the Japanese as *jjokbari*. This refers to the sandals they wore in the old days. The word *jjok* means piece and, as mentioned previously, *bal* means foot, so the whole word literally means "a piece of a foot." Why a piece of a foot? Their straw shoes were not really complete shoes, not even slippers; they were sandals, in that they had only a sole and no chassis. This is in contrast, of course, to the Korean straw shoe, which completely enclosed the foot. So, as the glass shoe identified Cinderella, in the *jo-o-ri*, which is what the Japanese call this sandal, we can see the possibility of some comparative relationship between Japanese culture and the shoes they wore.

Let us, then, try a comparison between the Japanese and the Korean. They share one point in common in that both the *jo-o-ri* of the Japanese and the *jipshin* of the Koreans were made of straw, by hand. That is where the similarity ends. The form and the technical design show a conspicuous difference, as described just above. In a word, we might say the jo-o-ri is only the sole of a shoe, and so it must have some kind of strap to keep it on the foot. Its simple design is due to the fact that they knew how to design only that much, and so they had no choice but to wear this sandal, like it or not. The Korean shoe, on the other hand, was made from the same straw, but the straw was woven in an intricate, sophisticated way that provided complete coverage of the foot, and included a heel at that. When you consider the fact that the Korean shoe and the Japanese slipper were made not by some craftsman but in the servants' quarters, you can get some idea of the comparative skills of the Koreans and the Japanese, and the beginnings of their sense of design.

For it is not only in production skills but also in their sense of design that Koreans are so distinguished. In the Korean shoe, made of wood, straw or rubber, you will find the heart of the shoe in the toe. All the shoe's lines and its whole texture flow from every part to meet together here at this one point. The toe of the straw shoe is actually a hole. All the beauty of the straw shoe flows through its lines and weave to finally gather at that one circle of emptiness.

In Korea's wooden shoe, too, in its rubber shoe, and even in its boot sock, along their lines also flows that elemental force inherent in any matter (which we call *ki*). One would expect there to be quite a commotion when the forces coursing in from every part of the shoe converge here at this one point. But the toe of the Korean shoe is so designed that these forces are dissipated and not allowed to concentrate into a coherent mass, which would harden that area.

The aesthetic in that high rounded toe of most Korean shoes, and in the empty toe of the straw shoe, is the embodiment of Korean culture. Call it an emancipating culture if you will, there is clear evidence of it here in the toe of our shoes. The process involved in turning bulky straw into the delicate, intricately woven straw shoe employs the distinctive features of the Korean's simple-hearted but sensitive character.

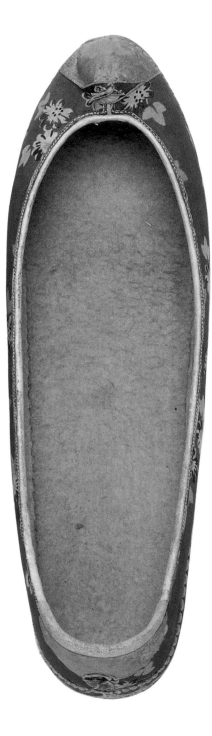

Relaxing Wrestling

씨름

Ssirum

One folk painting by the classical artist Hye-won depicts a scene from *ssirum*, the traditional Korean wrestling match. Two big bruisers are locked in a knot of torsos and limbs, and it is very difficult to predict who will come out the winner. A crowd of spectators is gathered round the ring, and it seems from the intensity of their attention that there might be some money bet on this match.

The painting has a kind of a cartwheel composition to it, with the wrestlers forming the axle and the surrounding audience forming the spokes. Its taut lines and the intent expression on the face of each one viewing the bout give the scene an acute tension you do not often find in classical paintings.

But there is relief to this tension provided by the taffy man at the edge of the crowd. The attention of the spectators is riveted on the wrestlers, and the taffy man is looking at the spectators. So the wrestlers are watching each other, and the audience is watching the wrestlers, and the taffy man is watching the audience. Each human element has a distinct look in his eye—the wary look of the wrestlers, the thrilled looked of the spectators, the meandering look of the taffy man—so that there is no one single ambience to the painting. The closer in toward the center you are, the stronger the tension, and the farther out your eye travels from the center, the more the tension diffuses. Into the middle of all that stifling tension the casual clanking of the taffy man's shears stirs a smile, a refreshing breeze of comic relief.

That is what Korean wrestling is. In some other forms of wrestling the action is all over in a flash, before you realize the match has even begun. This is especially true of Japanese sumo, where everything is decided in an instant, like a cock fight. The longest sumo match is all over in the first round. In Korean ssirum just getting started takes longer than, and provides as much fun as an entire sumo match. First there is all that fidgeting to get the thigh strap on just right; when they finally set their chins into each other's right shoulder and clutch the other's thigh straps in the get-set position, then begins that endless subtle nudging and maneuvering, and sometimes even breaking and starting the process all over again, for the best grip and most advantageous stance. With all this stalling just to get started it may seem the first couple seconds will determine the whole match, but, unlike in sumo, this is only the first of several rounds. So the spectator can sit back and enjoy himself.

The first one to hit the ground is the loser of the round, but occasionally it is quite difficult to tell who hit the ground first. So the one judged the loser has a lot to say. This is another feature of Korean ssirum. The outcome might not always be fair, but at least the loser always has the opportunity to save some face. He will complain either about the other's thigh strap, or how his opponent started off too soon, or whatever else he can come up with. If it were not for this the contest would have that cold, heartless finality of big-time sports.

The proper adjustment of the thigh belt, though an important ritual, is not as strictly regulated as weighing the gloves in a boxing match. And, as mentioned before, the accuracy of the referee's decision as to who hit the ground first is often suspect. But this ambiguity is at least subconsciously expected, an essential element of the game. In fact, this absence of fastidiousness is one of the most attractive aspects of ssirum.

In life the amount of stress one suffers is in direct proportion to the amount of responsibility he takes on. And lots of responsibility can often mean a sense of loneliness. Consider the goalkeeper in a soccer game, or a hockey game—the outcome often seems to depend entirely on him, and one can feel his loneliness out there by himself in front of that goal. In contrast, when one has taken on little responsibility his heart is light and free.

In ssirum you can see both a degree of tension and a degree of leeway in both the wrestler and the spectator. The ssirum wrestler, despite his determination, is allowed by the more casual nature of the game not to get all keyed up over some sense of responsibility, and so does not feel that loneliness of the goalkeeper. The spectator knows this, and can sit back and enjoy a satisfying blend of tension and comic relief.

A Rule-of-Thumb Kite
연
Yonz

A poet wrote, "And I felt that same nostalgia for Heaven." After all, heaven is our real home, where we really came from. We Koreans also feel nostalgia for our rectangle kite, with that hole in the middle that lets us see our old home. Tipped red or black, there is that half moon at its top and those tails flapping at the bottom corners of the skirt. This is the kite we used to fly in our youth, that kite that flew so nicely in the deep blue winter sky high above the elm in the yard, over the thatch roof of our home.

This was the rectangle kite, and we all used it, so we did not even bother to give it a name. We just called it "the kite."

What they call a kite in the West has no hole in its center. We can see in that illustration of Benjamin Franklin flying his kite that they like the stingray kite. And the popular one in Kansai Province in Japan is the cuttlefish kite (they call it *ikka*), much like the stingray kite.

Then why would Koreans be the only ones to prefer a kite with a hole in it? Well, all we have to do to get the answer is think back to when we flew those kites as kids. When you fly a kite like the stingray, without the hole, you have to be a master flyer or you will not even get off the ground. The kite is designed so intricately that, even if you do finally manage to get it up, the slightest slip will send it into a fatal nosedive.

But the Korean kite, with its hole, always manages to fly, even if it is crudely made, and does not go and lose its balance once you get it flying. If it starts trailing off to the left, just give some line on the right, and do the same on the left if you want to stop it veering to the right. And you can control it even better by pulling in and letting out its head line. So no matter how poorly made the kite is, if you just work the strings right everyone will think you have the magic touch.

The special feature of the Korean kite, then, is that it is makeshift; it is not complete in itself from the beginning, but gradually achieves completeness during its flight, as its flyer compensates with some slack here and a tug there. The stingray kite symbolizes that culture which plans and calculates in intricate detail, while the Korean kite symbolizes the culture which goes easy on the planning and compensates during operation.

It is often noted about Koreans that they go too much with the "rule of thumb" principle. But when you have superior reflexes and the flexibility to rectify as you go, who needs such fastidious attention to detail before anything even thinks of happening?

Look at the stingray kite through a Korean's eye, and you can not help seeing something rigid and hidebound. The Korean knows how to make a rule-of-thumb kite fly, by simply cutting a hole in its center.

Coin of Universal Tender
엽전
Yopjon

There is an anecdote from ancient China which clearly suggests something about what we might call our realm of value. The story goes that one time a sage of Ch'i China loses his bow in the mountains, and when someone asks him why he does not go out and look for it, the sage asks why he should look for something which is not lost—it would have to be somewhere in China. Everyone gasps at this profound insight into the concept of how far out one will reach in identifying with oneself. But then Confucius walks up and says, "Why only China? Why not humanity?" And just about when everyone is finished recovering from their dumbfounded shock of greater awe at this more widely encompassing wisdom, Lao-tzu comes along and speaks his piece. "Humanity? How about the cosmos?"

The ordinary man's realm of value is restricted to that which he knows personally and directly. What he does not have direct experience with has no real value to him. With those of broader mind, this realm can extend to the borders of the nation, and with yet others it can transcend national boundaries to include all of humanity. And some can even transcend humanity, to embrace the entire cosmos, all of existence.

Because of the influence of Lao-tzu's Taoism, which extends this realm to the very edge of the cosmos, much is included in the Asian realm of value. Thus, in terms of material interest, much is done here which can be regarded as impracticable. This is true even with our coin, that human device most closely identified with material interest.

The designs of the old Korean coin and the coin of the West are basically different. The Korean coin was a round sphere with a square hole in its center. Its roundness signified the sky, and the square hole in the center signified the four compass points of the Earth. So, in spite of its small size, it belonged to the entire universe.

Western coins, with their engraving of the nation's sovereign, show a contrast to the old Korean coin. The value of the coin is determined by worldly power, in the name of the sovereign. Visualize Caesar's image on the Roman coin, and you can feel directly that even Jesus recognized the authority of the image on that coin when he said, "Render unto Caesar what is Caesar's..." The god who created the value of that coin was a human, the one whose image was impressed on it.

Even if something is of worldly value the Asian uses it in accordance with the principles which order the universe. Koreans did not think the form of their coin sufficiently displayed its full philosophical import, so on the coin, in Chinese characters, they imprinted such philosophical messages as "Universal tender." In this way, the old Korean coin carried the most philosophical and religious meaning of all currencies on the face of the earth.

At the same time, this old coin was of the most practical design, because it had that square hole in the center which allowed one to string a lot of these coins together. Such a design obviated any treasure chest or money sack which would otherwise be needed for carrying a sizable number of these coins.

We might say the coin of western Europe, imprinted with a face and a value, is practical. In that sense, then, the old Korean coin was abstract and conceptual. Because the western coin is practical, if the government which issued it were to cease, the coin would lose its value. But this was not so with the old Korean coin—it had nothing to lose, even if the kingdom or the humans using it were to disappear. Its value did not change with the wax and wane of empire. It had inherent philosophical value, and this gave the simple iron ore which constituted it a primal universal value. And this, in turn, gave it an independent intrinsic value.

The old Korean coin, originally of the uni-

verse, has returned to the universe. For this very reason it retains a transcendental value limited only by the boundaries of the universe.

A Game for Only the Strong of Heart

윷

Yut

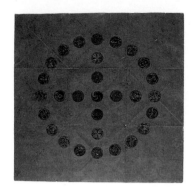

When we play any game we employ the element of risk. In fact, the Korean word for gamble (*norum*), the activity most heavily influenced by probability, comes from the verb for play (*nold-da*). The more risk involved, the more thrilling the game will be. The opposite of a game of risk is programmed activity, such as working on an assembly line; this kind of activity is enervating, and there are many things of this nature which we would not do if we did not get paid for it. With a game like cards, on the other hand, even if we lose money we want to keep on playing all night.

Of course, there are many games which do not require betting. Of all such games, Korea's board game, *yut*, is the most exciting. The game board has only to appear, and the level of energy in the room jumps. It is a free-for-all until the game is over.

If we compare it with the dice that Westerners like so much we can see why everyone gets so much more excited in a game of yut. Considering the factor of probability it would seem that dice must be more interesting, because in yut there are only five possible numbers (determined by how the four playing sticks land), whereas in dice there are at least six. But in the actual process of the game it is a different story. Once you throw that one die everything is decided in a split second, and the players know their fate right away. But in yut there is suspense. You do not know what you are getting into until all the sticks have finally decided whether they are going to rest face up or face down. Sometimes this decision takes what seems an eternity, lasting until all the sticks finally settle. Though the degree of probability is less here than in the game of dice, there is that much more anxiety, because the uncertainty is prolonged. It is like in a detective story, in which uncertainty is artfully played for all it is worth to mystify and build up the suspense to its greatest pitch.

So the excitement of yut is in the sticks' delaying tactics. Dice, even with its minimum of six possible numbers, has none of this. It is not only because of that lack of any hint as to which way the sticks will fall that yut is so captivating, but also because of the way it employs the factor of suspense to an even greater degree through both its regulations and the layout of the board.

The board is bordered with an equal number of spots, equivalent to the squares in western board games, on each of its four sides. One of the four players has to make it around the board in order to win the game. How many spots you advance depends on how the sticks land—the combination of sticks face up or face down—when tossed. Whether you have to go all the way around the board or get to take a shortcut (along the lines which connect diagonal corners) depends on whether or not you are lucky enough to get a combination in the toss which lands you on a corner spot. You could get one of your pieces "home" in one turn, or you could take several turns and never get home. Then there is the most frustrating case when, having taking several turns to go around the longest way, you are just about to get home when you are "eaten" by another player landing on that spot you tried so hard to get to. Which means, of course, that you must start all over again. So on one hand you could be very lucky and get the highest possible combination in several successive tosses, but at the same time miss the shortcut gates at the corners because of this prolific luck; and it is not such a rare occurrence that this same "luck" keeps you on the board and ultimately costs you the game. So your progress depends on the lay of the board and on the toss of the sticks. Life's whims are much more influential than your navigational skills.

Then again, the stylish contortions some go through in tossing their sticks make one think there may be at least some element of control over how the sticks fall. One never knows, and this adds to the fun.

Kaiowa analyzed the nature of games and came up with four features: competition, risk, thrill and imitation. Yut incorporates every one of these features. The special ways players have of tossing the sticks arouses a keen atmosphere of competition. We find the feature of risk in that sense we have, at the beginning of the game, of stepping into a sword fight or a wrestling match. And the layout of the board and the regulations of the game give it an element of risk equal to gambling, in which one's fate is determined by the fickle moods of Lady Fortune. We thrill at the way the players simply cannot sit in one place, and will suddenly jump up into a dance or shout out in agony or ecstasy. Imitation is the most subtle of these four features, but you can see it nevertheless in the names, derived from Chinese characters, of the combinations in the stick toss.

You get a pig, lowest in value, when the planed side of one stick and the rounded side of three sticks are up, and you can move ahead only one square. You can get a dog, a sheep or an ox (which is also the name of the game). Or you may get a horse, which is the best possible toss because you can move ahead five squares. Some are of

the opinion that the assignment of names for the different combinations was originally determined by the speed at which each of the animals moves, the fastest, of course, permitting the player to advance the most squares. Description of progression, too—whether the player takes the long way around or one of the short cuts—is a reflection of the sun of the summer solstice (the long way, naturally) and the winter solstice, and also the movement of other heavenly bodies.

In accordance with the transpositional opposition inherent in yin and yang, we get the planed half of the stick or its rounded half up or down; this is yut's langue, its conventions. And in the movement of the pieces we have yut's parole, the employment of those conventions. Would it, after all, be going too far to see in yut an embodiment of Sausseur's structural linguistics and its system of symbols?

A word of warning: If you have a weak heart, you would be well advised to leave your house when someone brings out the yut board.

Cushions and Bedding That Will Floor You
이불과 방석
Ibul and Bangsok

The bed in the West monopolizes that one place in the room, whether someone is sleeping in it or not. Even when the one who uses it is up and about his work outside, the bed lies there by itself, taking up its own space. The vastness of Versailles was designed around the bed of Louis XIV. And the first thought of Odysseus, upon his return home, was not of his wife, but of his bed, as we can see in the scene where he rages at Penelope for allowing his bed to have been moved from its original position of more than ten years before.

Modern devices exist independently of us. There is no difference, therefore, between the innocuous bed and Frankenstein, another of our devices. Is it any wonder that the modern conveniences that we have created for our comfort cause us grief in the end?

The sleeping mat and quilt of Korea, on the other hand, serve and delight the one using them. They can be folded up and tucked neatly away in a small space after we are finished with them. Our bedding gets up with us. And so space in the house does not exist for the devices in it, but for the people who inhabit it.

Space in a western house is planned for and around its devices, and the house ends up with furniture space and people space. In a traditional Korean house, on the other hand, the space is tiered, to serve with maximum efficiency the various and simultaneous needs of all those living there. Want to sleep? Roll out the mat and quilt. Want to eat? Roll up the mat, move it over a bit, and bring in the floor table.

In the West when they get up from a chair, the chair keeps sitting there taking up all that space for itself. Look at the easy chair. Its owner gone, it just goes on lounging comfortably there, in all its arrogance, taking up all that room for itself and its splendid arms and towering back. It seems as if the western living room exists for these chairs to get a nice rest.

In the opinion of someone who regards things in the way a Korean does, there is nothing more stuffy in its self-esteem than a chair. The floor cushion, the Korean equivalent of the western chair, is there when you want to sit, and then gets up with you, leaving not a trace of itself, when you get up.

Then there is the matter of appearance. No matter how cheap or how expensive the western armchair, what you see when you chance to look underneath is always the same jungle of springs and dangling ends. There is no messier place than the bottom of a bed or chair. The bottom of the Korean sleeping mat, though, is also its top—whether the surface you see right now is top or

bottom depends on whether the mat is in use or not. At night, the top is the fresh cotton surface you sleep on. In the morning, when you get up and fold the mat away properly, what was its underside now becomes its top, an embroidered surface of resplendent patterns and colors. Fold it this way or that way to display that aspect of its pattern which catches your fancy. It is a revolving exhibition of art, a sculpture wrought anew day to day in reflection of your every mood.

We can get some sense of the poignant beauty of the Korean quilt in the lines of the courtesan-poetess Hwang Jin-i: "Fold by happy fold when he's to come, fold by loving fold when he's left." A kind of bed, you might say, but one which reflects what its master is doing.

Wardrobe Mosaic
장농
Jangnong

We think of the wardrobe as a place to hang our clothes. But it would be more accurate to speak of Korea's traditional wardrobe as a place to pile clothes.

In Korea's wardrobe the clothes are folded and stacked on top of each other. That is why, when we look inside, we sometimes feel we are looking down into the depths of a well. Indeed, when we step back and observe those clothes piled on top of each other, we are reminded of the earth's geological strata. We might equate the deepest layer, way at the bottom, with the earth's core, and the top of the stack with the earth's surface.

Each layer has its own special nature. In the summer, the layer way down at the bottom is winter clothing, but after a few months has passed, look again—now the summer clothing is buried down there. And the layers in the middle will hold clothing for the more temperate months. So the strata revolve according to the revolution of the seasons.

It is not only seasonal change that determines what is on the floor of the wardrobe. The very difficulty involved in pulling something out from way down inside there affords a place to secure the family's valuables. Embedded in the deepest fathoms of the wardrobe we will find the anchor which stabilizes and secures the family through the storms that life will now and then send its way.

That is why, though the Korean wardrobe is not all that high, its depth is an abyss. One cannot locate the valuables stored in the wardrobe simply by opening it up and looking inside. The clothing covering these valuables has to be taken out, piece by piece. The Korean wife or mother looking for some valuable can resemble some prospector digging away shovel by shovel, or the pearl diver pushing down, down and around among the coral reefs. Whether it be a worn out piece of clothing or some yellowing family photo, each item uncovered during the search receives a special greeting in the mother's smile, or in her sigh. This welcome can sometimes come close to the exclamations an archeologist will utter in the process of excavating an ancient tomb. In the depths of the wardrobe are things lost to time, forgotten in life's forced march, naturally receiving a special welcome when they surface again and beckon us to stay a bit and remember.

This stratified structure is inherent in every Korean chest no matter what kind or size of chest it is. It does not have to be a full-sized wardrobe. It may be the chest for boot socks, which looks like a child's minia-

ture of the larger wardrobe, but has that same indeterminable depth. Whether it is a chest divided into several compartments, like the wardrobe, or of just one cavity with nothing more than its floor to serve as its one and only "shelf," any Korean chest has its layers and its bottomless bottom.

The wardrobe does not come in only one size or type. The feature which best distinguishes one wardrobe from another is the number of levels it has, and we name them accordingly. There is the two-shelf wardrobe, the three-shelf wardrobe, and so on. As the eye follows these shelves up or down, as it alights on each of the shelves and on the layers of clothing stacked on them, one begins to sense a regular rhythm there. Then again, in each wood shelf nature provides an irregular pattern in the grain of the persimmon tree or the paulownia. We can see in this regular rhythm and irregular pattern the beauty of a mosaic, and this mosaic is enhanced by the varied patterns and colors of the clothes stacked several high on each shelf.

The Korean wardrobe is a composition of a simple rhythm weaving colors and textures into a mosaic of life. Though its contents are not locked up as if in a safe, they are protected from prying hands by the wardrobe's ever revolving depths. Never

locked, in its fathomless depths it nevertheless safeguards its most precious things, as does the heart of the Korean mother.

The Condiments Bay

장독대

Changdokdae

The woman of traditional Korea cares for both her appearance and her family. She tends to her appearance at the dressing table. And at the condiments bay she tends to her family. After all, we do have that old proverb, "If you want to know a household, try its condiments."

On the dressing table are neatly placed all her cosmetics powders, hair dressings, fragrances. And in the food stocks bay out in the yard are lined, just as neatly, rows of all different shapes and sizes of crocks of kimchi, soybean paste, hot pepper sauce and other condiments.

The essential element in the taste of Korean food is the condiments used in it as seasoning or served along with the meal on the table, which means that the basic taste of the food of a household is determined by how the condiments are prepared. Such an essential thing cannot be determined only by the skills the housewife may have in her fingertips. The taste of her condiments depends much more on the devotion in her heart. No matter how expertly the ingredients for the condiments are selected and blended, if something goes wrong during the fermentation process all that expert skill will come to naught. So fermentation demands constant, devoted attention. On a sunny day the lid must be open to let in the sun, and on a rainy day it must be closed to keep out the rain. The housewife has to keep one eye constantly on the condiments bay, because if she does not, she cannot expect the condiments to turn out properly. This is why we say that a woman who has her eye on the condiments bay is one who has her family in her heart. And that is why we also say that we can taste the quality of her devotion and love for her family in the condiments she makes.

We can also tell how she regards a guest. In the traditional household, rich or poor, there is always one crock hidden way back in the furthest corner. The condiments for the most honored guests are in that guarded nook.

The intriguing thing about this bay is that, while it harbors an essential of the household, it is never secured with lock and key, like a shed or cabinet can be. And it is not enclosed, like the wine cellar in the West. It is out in the open—it has to be, in fact, to get the sun and fresh air. Still, the condiments bay is always located in an out-of-the-way place, in the backyard; after all, there is no need to tempt anyone. It is not secured, but it is not displayed, either. So we might see in this a poetic duality of harmony in contradiction. The condiments bay is open even as it is closed.

In the traditional family, when the new wife's life under the thumb of Mother-in-law gets too hard, she will let go a few tears in the comforting recesses of the condiments bay. The condiments bay of old Korea—a very tranquil place, where the dragon fly drops in on the touch-me-not, and time stops for a rest. And the bulging condiment crocks sit there quietly processing the family's sustenance.

Totem Couple
장승
Changsung

Just a few decades ago, at the approach to any village, at the top of a pass near the hushed, solitary shrine to the local deity, and along any country road where they served also as a milepost, there was that totem couple. No matter how difficult the characters in the weathered and decaying wood were to decipher you could always somehow make out the faint impression of the Chinese characters identifying the "Guardian of the World Above," and his mate, "Guardian of the World Below." They are also commonly thought of in terms of the guardians of heaven and earth.

At the base of this totem couple was always a pile of stones. The traveler with a special wish would put the wish in a stone and place the stone at the feet of this couple. Year by year the pile would grow, to evolve into a shrine of the simple people.

We can see the totem couple nowadays in our bustling cities, erected mainly for foreign tourists. But what could the tourist see in them?

And what, after all, is it that the Korean sees in them? Let's start with their posture. The standing figures appear as two pillars. They reflect the basic desire of the human to go through life in an upright manner. This yearning is first felt by the human being in his toddler stage, and he does not know it

then but this yearning is ultimately the instinct to stand strong and erect, like a pillar, with feet solidly on the ground and head in the sky. This is man acting upon his primal memory of those oldest of myths which told of when heaven and earth were in close correspondence.

Maybe this will help us understand how these totems came to be mates. The male is guardian of heaven and earth–this life–and the female is guardian of the subterranean, the netherworld. Another way of regarding them, though, is the male as sky and the female as soil. No matter how we see them, they are both guardians in one universe, mates in the governance of life.

This unity of heaven and earth in two mates, one couple, reminds one of the mating and reproduction process of two individual gingko trees. Like the gingko tree, which reproduces through interaction with the opposite gender, the totem couple signifies renewal of the natural order through interaction of their different realms.

In this desire which we see in the totem couple to live upright and to be with one's mate, we see the spirit of the Korean. A tree dies not simply from the wound it receives when it is chopped down by the ax. It really dies because it is no longer erect, when it finds itself supine, no longer itself but some carpenter's lumber. And it is the same with a Korean, who is felled and dies when the mate is lost.

The disappearance of the totem couple from our midst signifies the disappearance of upright living and loss of our mate. We live in an era in which the moon and the stars are gone, a time in which the pollinating butterfly and the conjugal mandarin ducks have died.

When these guardians stood at the entrance to every village we saw in these proud figures heaven's participation in our existence. When the earth became soaked in the rain falling from above we thrilled to think that heaven and earth were one. The people of those times were like the totem couple in the way those two guardians maintained the universal life principle of yin and yang.

The Temple Bell

종

Jong

There are not many of man's creations which show better the contrast between East and West than the bell.

While the large inverted-tulip western bell, used from about the twelfth century, is rung from the inside, which requires that its whole casing be moved in order to ring it, the eastern bell remains stationary, because it is rung from the outside with a wooden hammer. Because the whole thing has to move to produce its ring, the size of the western bell is limited.

The temple bell of the East, therefore, can be made much bigger than the western bell. While everything in the West is made on a big scale, its bell is not.

Look at the western bell through the eyes of a Korean, who has produced the world famous Bulguk Temple's Emille Bell. This bell boasts a height of 3.78 meters and a diameter of a little over 2 meters. When the Korean hears or sees a bell of the West he might well be reminded of a hand bell, or a jingle bell. Rabelais' Gargantua was supposedly so big that he used the cathedral's bell on his horse. In the land of the Emille Bell it would not take a giant to carry such a tinkler.

In lieu of great size western bells often come in groups of different sizes, with which they call produce a melody of different tones. While the western bell can produce melody the eastern temple bell, because of its size, can produce majestic tone with lasting reverberation. To produce a ring with the western bell a metal tongue is struck against the inner metal casing; the sound of metal on metal is light and shallow and has a shorter resonance. The temple bell is struck with a wooden hammer, and when wood strikes the right kind of metal we hear a deep sound whose reverberation continues on and on.

Among all the bells of the East, Korea's temple bell best represents the character of the East. This is because the Korean bell, for fuller and longer reverberation, has an original design distinct from the Japanese and Chinese bells. Its chimney-like flu at the top (which controls the tone), its thirty-six knobs, nine each in four blocks spaced equally around the bell's shoulder, and the large earthenware vessels under the bell—all of these features enhance the bell's resonance and reverberation.

From the form of the Korean temple hell with its reliefs of flying devas we get an impression of the conveyance of human supplications all the way to heaven. It was believed that with the ringing of the temple bell we would be released from the snares of the 108 tribulations and oppression by supernatural powers and evil, and be absolved of our sins to boot. In its deep significance this bell is basically different from the western bell, which has more the nature of a watchman's rattle than anything else.

The Japanese, so proud of the exalted casting method which made their swords famous throughout the world, could never hope to produce anything like the bell of Korea. The Koreans, having produced as early as the eighth century the world's biggest bronze bell, were clumsy at producing things which take life, but have yet to find their equal at producing that resonating ring which saves souls.

A-Frame: Aesthetics at Work
지게
Jige

The origin of the word *jige* is the verb *ji-da*, to carry on one's back. Just as *topgae*, the Korean word for bed cover, originates in *top-da*, to cover, and *begae* (a pillow) comes from *be-da*, which is to rest one's head on a pillow. So the jige is a device for carrying things.

No other country has the jige. The Americans had to improvise a name for it—they call it the A-frame (not to be confused with the A-frame building), obviously because from the front it looks something like the letter A. When they carry something, they use only the shoulder or only the back, because they have no device similar to the jige to help them transport things. It is no wonder they have no really proper name for the jige.

No matter how complex and sophisticated a contraption, the human's devices for transport can be represented in two simple verbs: carry and pull. From these two concepts come the shoulder strap and the wheel.

From the wheel came the train and the automobile, and from the train and automobile came the airplane. And finally came the wheel's ultimate development, the rocket. From the shoulder strap later developed many devices for carrying, but, if my guess is right, the Korean jige is still the shoulder strap's ultimate development. Even in this

age of the computer we see primary school students carrying their books and lunch in their knapsacks, and soldiers in our modern missile-equipped armies still use backpacks. But these are limited in the amount they can carry, and they do not really amount to something one would call a device, anyway.

Not even the strongest weight lifter can lift three times his weight, but in Korea it is not unusual to see the commonest farmer and his jige carrying a few sacks of rice, several times his own weight, with no trouble at all. And we will occasionally see the man who gathers pine needles with his load towering over him at more than twice his height.

The secret is in their sense of balance and sense of rhythm, and the way they coordinate the two. With the jige, all you have to do is set the load off a little, and not even a Hercules could carry this load. The heavier the load, the more essential it is to get a rhythm, like the regular undulation of the waves, and keep it. In this sense the jige is like a musical instrument. Or you might compare it to the carpenter's level in measuring consonance, and the metronome in telling rhythm.

The jige viewed from the front looks like the letter A, but viewed at an angle it looks like two single-limbed trees with their tops resting against each other. So, from the side the A-frame becomes the Y-frame. Now look at the upper half of the Y, just the V part. That space between the two V's is the essence of the jige. This crevice carries the load.

The jige takes its basic form straight from nature. In the Y, you see the antlers of the buck, or maybe a forking creek. That space created by the V symbolizes the growth and proliferation of all living things.

We can feel a strong tension between the limbs and trunk. Just sling a band of rubber across the top, and the jige reminds us of the slingshot of our childhood.

The jige has a strength which we cannot find in the wheel. In the jige is the strength of a set of antlers, the ethereal beauty of the biceps.

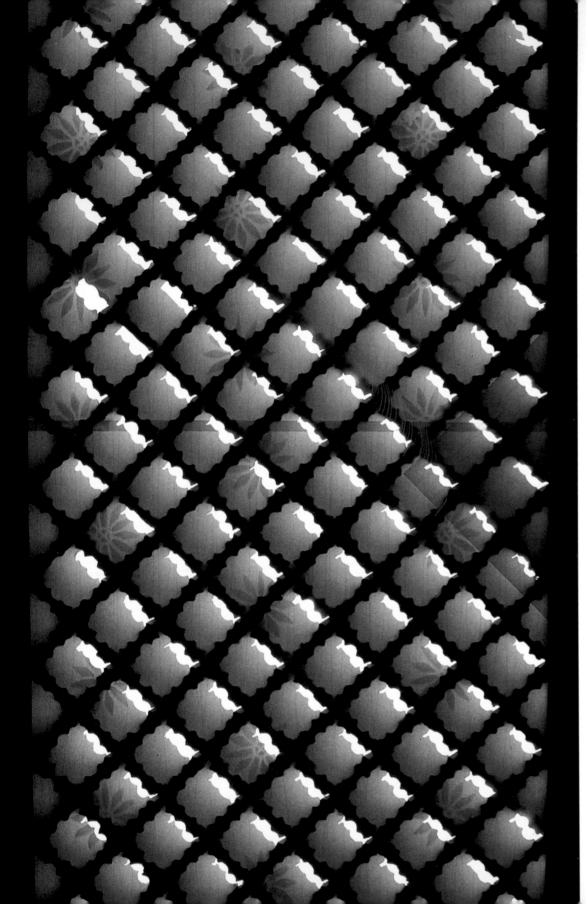

Living Window Paper
창호지
Changhoji

A Korean poet once wrote about the window,
"How this cold, sad thing does shine!" And
he described the heart of the person clean-
ing it as "lost in lonely contemplation." If
he had been born fifty years earlier he
would not have written this, for the glass
window was not common in his country.
The glass window is a product of the modern
age, and a very representative product
indeed.

The traditional Korean window is made of
rice paper, not of glass. Because of this it
gives off a feeling very much the opposite of
sadness and loneliness. The French writer
Jean Baudrillard described the tree as having "a warmth to it, so that it does not reflect
anything like glass does but glows from the
inside. The tree holds time in its fiber."
Though he was describing wood he could
just as well have been referring to the paper
of the Korean window. This window paper
is not "cold" but warm, and has no "shin-
ing" reflection but is imbued with shadows.
It is not something which is cleaned, but is
rather left to flavor with age. And so the
rice paper window is not a "sad" thing;
rather, it offers a pleasing intimacy. This
paper, made from pliant wood, in terms of
yin and yang has a character which is the
polar opposite of the mineral-based glass
window.

The difference between the glass window and the paper window is the difference between tradition and modernity, the difference between East and West.

We can make an analogy to illustrate this. There are two poles, one of glass in the realm of intellect, and the other of window paper in the realm of emotion. The intellect is like glass, clear, hiding nothing, in fact exposing whatever it can. That is why the room with a glass window lets in all the light and shows every speck of dust, every flaw. Window paper blocks about half of the light, casting the room in a dim shade, hiding the dust and eliminating the flaws. The crackle glaze porcelain of the early Chosun dynasty, displayed in museums throughout the world, shows its true quality in the filtered light which window paper provides. In the glare of daylight it may appear as no more than a badly cracked piece of pottery.

When a glass window breaks, it is all over for that window. Even a little crack will compromise its basic function. Window paper, on the other hand, does not break. It may tear, it may get a puncture in it. But like living, breathing organic skin, the wound does not stay, it mends.

The intellect is oriented toward the absolute and the abstract, both of which have no use for time. If you clean a piece of

glass you clean away the grime of time. Time simply does not stick to glass. Glass does not decay, it does not discolor. But with window paper, the more years roll by the more of time's moss it gathers, and the richer its color. It changes, it wears away, and then it dies. The glass window breaks; the paper window returns to its elements.

The emotions of the heart are not as tough as the ideas of the intellect. The emotional is fluid, not something solid like the intellect. Skin punctures and scratches more easily than the skull. Before you know it, though, the puncture or scratch mends; the skull is quite another problem.

Until a few decades ago Korean women softened and smoothed their family's laundry with a rhythmic pummeling of the laundry bat. The scene of a faint, flickering silhouette cast on the window paper is often used these days to evoke the spirit of traditional life in Korea. One begins to understand why.

The Roof's Hip

처마
Choma

It has often been said that the beauty of Korea is best appreciated in its concept of line. In distinguishing the nature of art in countries of the Far East the key words used are form for China, color for Japan, and line for Korea. And when they speak of Korea's concept of line the most frequently used example is the hip—the corner—of its tile roof.

Chinese, Japanese and Korean roofs all look generally the same, but the hip of the Korean roof is a smooth curve, not straight like the Chinese or Japanese. It is more than a curve, though. The hip swoops up toward the sky, giving the impression of soaring into it, as if this massive roof pressing down toward the earth is actually going to take off and fly. Imagine the swallow floating down to alight when, without the slightest break in rhythm, a sudden burst of its wings swoops him up into the sky.

To be exact, we might say that this is more the beauty of opposing dynamic forces than of form. Form expresses something more significant than itself. Any line manifests action, and this includes the various forces of direction, speed and gravity. We might even go so far as to say that nothing manifests the complex forces involved in human desire as accurately as the line.

The beauty of the Korean roof is found more in the distinctive line of its hip than in the simple lines of its ridge and ribs. It is so distinctive because in the hip we have the intersection of the vertical and the horizontal, where the descendant force and the ascendant force meet, a meeting of heaven and earth. The hip is where subconscious will succeeds in puncturing the surface of the consciousness.

The fountainhead of that suppressed will, that which empowers it finally to break through the massive downward pull of the roof, is the vibrant colors which decorate the eaves tucked up beneath the hip. They glow like the hottest embers there within the restrained earth and wood tones of the general building, and when one detects them he fully appreciates the brilliant rebellion of color that they are.

These colors are related to Korea's indigenous religion. Green is the color of wood, and relates to spring and the east; red, the color of fire, corresponds with summer and the south; yellow is the color of soil, and signifies the revolution of the seasons and the centrality of soil; white, the color of metal, tells of autumn and the west; and black is water's color, of winter and the north.

One look at these five bold, striking colors and you will know how distorted is the generalization that Koreans prefer sombre colors. In traditional Korean clothing we often see the equivalent element of the effusive indulgence of the eaves abiding in the temple's sombre restraint. The browns and greys and blacks and whites of the parent's clothes are ubiquitous, but there are also those bright stripes of our children's holiday clothes. And often tucked inside the parents' clothing is that gleaming jade pendant or richly embroidered purse.

The spirit of the Korean roof's hip is not restricted to the Korean roof. It is the spirit of the Korean people.

The Silk Lantern: Enhancing the Night
초롱
Chorong

A dinner party in any country is usually held at night. One difference between Korean and western dinner parties is that the first concern at a western dinner party is how to light it as bright as midday. It is very important that it seem like an extension of daylight hours, and so artificial lighting is used. That is where the huge, elaborate candelabrum and chandelier come from.

The Korean, in contrast, has a dinner party at night so that he can enjoy the night, and thinks that dark is needed for it to be night. There is no thought to somehow reproduce the light of the sun; the ideal light is the subdued light of the moon and stars. You can see this in the stone lantern which adorns the yard of many a big home or building. Its function is not to provide light, like the powerful western chandelier or garden light, but to symbolize light.

Even the Korean lanterns which actually produce light are basically like the stone lantern, which gives off no light. Whenever there is an outside dinner party the red and green silk gauze lanterns make their appearance. They are not there to provide light, but rather to contain the light. They are there to create a festive atmosphere. That is why they are designed as they are—even in daylight the bright red and green colors afford the same feeling of festivity.

Note its form. It is designed that way to block the light. All sides are covered with colored paper or silk so that the light inside does not escape. Only the very bottom is left open, the falling light gently stimulating the ground to elicit its reflection of natural hues.

This lantern gives off a modest light. It offers no challenge to daylight, nor does it envy daylight's power. Its sole purpose is to enhance the darkness of the night. That may sound paradoxical: Koreans light their lanterns at night not to extend day into night, but to make night more like night. The lantern produces from inside its silk gauze shade a hazy, dim, dreamy light just like the night gives us.

The silk lantern is not the only thing we use for lighting which may seem unscientific. We do not use reflectors or clear glass to enhance the power of the light from our lamps, we use materials and design to control the diffusion of the light.

But is that really unscientific? To the one who considers the matter thoroughly comes the inescapable conclusion that this principle transcends the scientific. The Korean lantern was designed to produce a faint, hazy light, like the light of night. The paradoxical stone lantern, which never lights, is probably the most ideal lantern that the Korean could ever imagine.

But is this really paradoxical? Koreans light their lanterns at night not to extend day into night, but to make night more like night. The lantern produces from inside its silk gauze shade a hazy, dim, dreamy light just like the night gives us.

We prefer cloud-filtered moonlight to the glare of a clear moon. And so we shroud our light with silk or paper, or our doors and windows with the wood of lattice work. We want to see not only the beauty which the day gives but the beauty of the night, too.

An Obliging Outfit for the Lady
치마
Chima

The word which would most accurately describe Korean traditional clothing is wrap, in that the loosely fitting material is practically wrapped on. Whereas western clothing is measured and cut to fit the body as closely as possible, Korean clothing is of more general measurements, which gives it the flexibility to fit well no matter how much the body changes from day to day.

In these pages we have already suggested the example of the traditional Korean trousers–if your waist expands you wear it looser, if your waist contracts you wear it tighter. The waist of these trousers, which comes with inches to spare, can be adjusted to fit just right simply by loosening or tightening its sash. The jacket, too, men's or women's, has its breast tie which, unlike the fixed buttons on its western equivalent, can be loosened and tightened as you like.

And so, when the body expands or contracts, it does not have to worry about its clothes. The clothes are designed in consideration of the person wearing them. It is the same with women's clothing. In English the bottom piece is called the skirt, but we ought to stick with the Korean word *chima*, because its basic principle is different from its counterpart in the West.

First, there is no waist size. Like the traditional trousers it comes in one size, and you put it on and wrap it around as loose or as tight as you wish. It is not actually a completed product when you buy it, because completion comes only when you put it on–rather, wrap it on–and your body finally gives it a definite size.

The chima has the same flexibility as Korean trousers. If it is too long you just wear it higher, and if it is too short you wear it a little lower. The waist is up under the jacket, so no one can tell the difference.

Clothing is not, after all, some manufactured tool that you buy in standard sizes and hope your body will fit. Not Korean clothing, anyway. It is a living thing that lengthens and shortens and expands and contracts, breathing along with the one wearing it. So it does not restrict or imprison the body.

Modern western clothes are designed with the intention of showing off the attractive features of the body wearing them. It is just the opposite with Korean clothes. They are designed to hide the flaws of the one wearing them, and do not expose the body's shortcomings like western clothes do. In a western skirt a woman would not be able to hide her bow-legged knees or some burn or scar, and a woman with small breasts will in fact look flat-chested if she does not wear a padded bra. This padded bra, in fact,

points up a contradiction in that western clothing, which is designed originally to expose the body, is in this case being used to hide it.

A Korean specialist in fashion design says that the way one dresses in Korean traditional clothing can make that person look taller or shorter, heavier or lighter. The short woman can draw the chima in and wear it a bit longer, and the tall one can let the chima out and wear it a bit shorter. If she is fat or skinny, if her neck is too short or too long, all she has to do is adjust her clothing this way or that to take care of her problem. She can wear the collar long and narrow to make her neck appear longer, or wear it wide and short to make her neck appear shorter.

The chima is designed not only to enhance the nice figure but also to help the figure not so fully blessed.

Knives and Daggers

칼

Kal

The Korean kitchen knife has to be the dullest looking knife in the world. The thick, stubby handle and clumsy line of the blade give one the impression it would have trouble slicing warm butter. Then there is the hue of its blade, which instead of the cold glint of something really sharp is the dull gray of an old piece of wood. An exaggeration? Just compare it with the Japanese sashimi knife, with its needle-sharp point and sleek, slender blade of icy clarity. Then you will begin to understand how very much the Korean kitchen knife looks like anything but a knife.

Koreans have always thought of the knife as a bad omen. That is why a sharp knife is never left anywhere around the house outside the kitchen. And it is taboo as a gift, since presentation of a knife is regarded as symbolic of severing a close relationship.

And so, while the knife was originally designed to cut things easily, Koreans make their knives to look as if they cannot cut anything. That is why our kitchen knife does not cut or slice. You might say it wears the object into two rather than severing it. We get over it and lean down on it and push forward and then drag it back, forward and back, in the same way one works a saw.

The lady's traditional ornamental dagger is even more useless. Instead of using it to hurt another the Korean woman carried it with her as a decorative accessory. It was originally intended not for the lady to use in defending herself against a man by inflicting injury on him; it was supposed to be used as an instrument to kill herself rather than let the man violate her. Even that, though, was more symbolic than anything else since the blade of this dagger, no matter how sharp it might be, was too short to deal any mortal wound. This knife, which could hurt neither its owner nor another, amounted to nothing more than a symbol of the woman's absolute determination to protect her chastity.

When the sorceress swings her sword in her exorcism she is not trying to destroy the evil spirit but to sever its hold on its victim. It is the same with religious leaders in Tibet, who use the swords they carry on them not to fight with others but to save people, by severing the chains of evil and the choking vines which block the path to truth.

Our kitchen knife and ornamental dagger manifest the degree to which Korean culture rejects the sword.

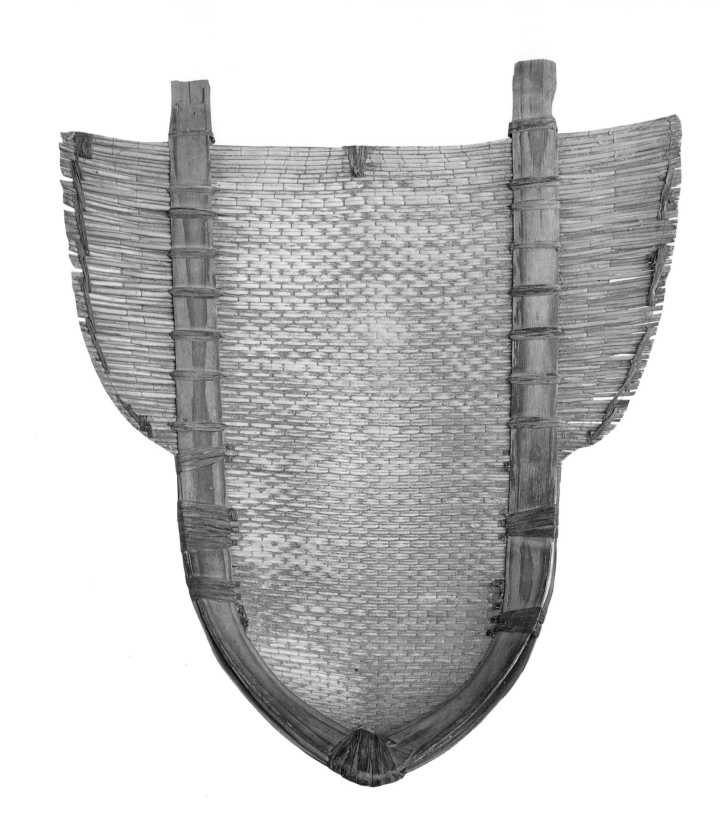

The Winnow: Dispersion and Cohesion

기

Ki

Among the utensils man has made, those which work in conjunction with the wind have a special beauty. This goes for the hand fan, the windmill, the kite, the wind vane...anything that either uses or creates wind. The sailboat is beautiful in the way its sails billow with the wind. On festival day we delight in the banners flapping in the wind, and our spirit rises even higher at the sight of all those colorful balloons. Then there is the stately dirigible, and the agile airplane. All these things which either produce wind or use it are like living creatures.

One of these beautiful creatures is the winnow. The winnow, like the airplane, manifests its uniquely beautiful form in its functioning, and its functioning in its form. With this we might say that this winnow achieves the culmination of beauty as a folk craft. That beauty is in the way it uses the organic combination of the decorative and the functional to achieve an ideal harmony of its two separate features of wings and belly.

With this winnow we toss the harvested grain in the air and let the wind carry off the chaff, and at the same time work the kernels heavy with ripeness to gather toward the inside. In order to get the chaff up into the wind you have to work the winnow's wings just right, in an outward, dispersing movement. You have to flap the wings, one at each edge, in perfect rhythm. At the same time the interior of the winnow must be worked in a way that it draws the grain inward, toward its belly.

So here is a complementary duet of dispersing with the wings while gathering with the belly. In this combination is the same tension you can see in the round toe of the Korean traditional shoe, which draws and brings to culmination in itself the force abiding in each line of the shoe's body.

I have emphasized it many times in these pages, but beauty, verbal or act, visual or audio, is the tension which develops in two opposites uniting. In the functioning of the winnow we can see the same aesthetic tension in that apparent incongruity in its separated wings acting in unison with its concentrated belly.

It used to be that when a Korean child wet his bed at night he was told to put a winnow on his head and go beg salt from the neighbors. The form of the winnow lent itself to this practice. The winnow's belly was a perfect fit on the head, and its back and wings made the whole thing look like a rain coat.

The Korean winnow is a continuing simultaneous movement of escaping gravity into the sky and yielding to gravity inward, a unity of separation and cohesion. The winnow is a visual synthesis of two dynamic forces. It is a boat with a magic sail, which both gathers and disperses the wind.

Dance of the Mask

탈

Tal

When we take a break from regular life for a while and throw a festival, we turn life on its head. Life's everyday plodding walk turns into a dance, the rice and water we drink day after day turn into rice cakes and aromatic wine. Our prosaic words become the stuff of rhythmic and melodic poetry and song. And our grimy, sweat-stained clothing turns into a brand new creation of bright patterns and gold tassels.

When everything changes abruptly like this we can compare it to putting on a mask. When work turns into play, when an everyday room becomes a banquet hall, when a way of life is turned around, this is like putting on a mask. And this masked face is not my face, not the one I usually see, anyway. It is a stranger's, or the ugly monk's or the happy Granny's of the traditional Korean mask dance.

If we were to equate the face with the lyrics of a song, a mask dance mask could be the rhythm and melody. Those faces we see everyday are rice and water, and the masked face is the intoxication of wine and the bean flour dressing on the rice cakes. The mask is the face's dance and party clothes.

One mask used in Japan's No theatre is famous for its inscrutably ethereal expression. It expresses neither happiness nor anger. No sorrow, no pain appear on that mask. This expressionless mask is the fixation of life in time, the human form in suspended animation, its reduction to something outside of existence.

The mask of Korea effects just the opposite. It maximizes human emotions and expressions and shows the wearer to be living life at its fullest. It is not easy for us to see in daily life the hearty laughter which lights the face of the mask dance Granny, nor that liquor-darkened face of the monk P'almok. We do not have it in us to scowl with those narrow slits the Scowler has for eyes, nor shock others with the outrageous ugliness of the Scabface Monk.

The world of the mask is a fun house mirror of life. This convoluted mirror, in the way it swells and shrinks and generally distorts, shows us the other side of life, another real side. The mask of the mask dance deprives the nobleman and the monk of old of their authority and exposes their hypocrisy. They are shown exactly for what they are. We undress them with this mask. On the other hand, the common man can see his potential—and what he really is—in this mask. When the plodding walk of everyday life is suspended and everything follows a new order like this...then the dancing begins.

One element in the mask dance is the mask, and the other is the dance. The dance is a take-off on the way we usually walk. We usually extend our right hand when we take a step with the left foot, and when we take a step with the right foot our left hand comes forward. But in the mask dance the right hand goes up with the right foot and the left hand goes up with the left foot. This is all highly stylized, of course, since it is dance. If anyone tried this on the street he would be stared at as an idiot. Those who are conquering and plundering in their headlong rush for power never walk this way. And if an army ever moved this way it would march right into annihilation.

This unique kind of walk is permitted—expected, in fact—only in the festival and the fun house mirror, where we free ourselves of the fetters and tribulations of our everyday world. And where we get a refreshingly different look at what the world is.

Taekwondo: Art in Motion

태권
Taekwon

The Chinese writer Lin Yu Tang once said that a western painting is touched and retouched, scraped and touched again, becoming in the end a work of many layers. This is in strong contrast to Far East painting. In Far Eastern ink painting there is no such thing as trial and error. Mistakes are not forgiven, there is no allowance for second thoughts. As in calligraphy, once the stroke is made, that's it. A mistake means the painting is done for, a change of mind means starting anew.

This comes to mind when we see taekwondo, for it can be the same in sport as in art. Compare taekwondo and boxing, for instance. Boxing is like painting in the West: the punches fly from bell to bell, but how many of these punches land on the opponent where they were intended to land? Taekwondo, though, is a silent stalking...then a sudden pounce.

Movement in taekwondo is considered and restrained. But when it happens it is instant and decisive. It resembles the process of calligraphy, where everything is accomplished in one flowing stroke, a sustained line, and there is no stopping to think on the way. There are no messy pokes, no tentative sparring, no grappling. It is one clean burst of unbroken movement.

The moves in taekwondo and calligraphy have other points in common. The beauty of taekwondo is the dynamic tension of a powerful but controlled line. In taekwondo there are several formal moves basic to the acquisition of the offensive and defensive skills, each move a standardized unit of several arm and leg movements. These moves, based on certain Chinese characters, are graceful in their liquid swiftness.

The first-degree black belt will step through each stroke in the character for a scholar (士), a third degree black belt will move through the character for build (工), and so on. We see in another standard move the Chinese character for eternity (永), which also happens to be drawn time after time by calligraphy neophytes in their quest of feel for line.

The beauty of form which we see in taekwondo is not simply a matter of arms and legs. It is also the product of the spirit inherent in the Chinese characters. That is why even one who knows absolutely nothing of the formal moves can still see in the standard side kick and the fore kick that miracle on silk of the transformation of the brush's trace into a living vine.

There is no difference between the movements in taekwondo and the lines of captured time in an ink painting. Here also we behold the stroke which is made once and for all, where the hand, once extended, and the foot, once raised, do not hesitate or vacillate or repeat or correct themselves in mid-movement. This is the absolute act seeking neither forgiveness nor a second chance.

Anyone, when it is all or nothing, will gird himself and concentrate his whole self on the task at hand. He is going to give all the strength in his body and soul to make this one and only stroke do its job. Here is found an elemental beauty which has nothing to do with the possibility of correction.

Yin-Yang's Cartwheel
태극
Taeguk

Traditional western cosmology sees the universe as consisting of three realms, heaven, hell and earth. The cosmology of the Far East has three realms, too, but that is where the similarity ends. In the Far Eastern view of the universe the three realms are heaven, earth and man.

Inside the vast system of this universe exist countless numbers of small universes, all homologous to each other since they are of the same system. This system is based on the yin-yang principle, an inherent part of the Far Eastern consciousness since the beginning of our civilization.

The principle of yin-yang is that life is governed by the interaction of two opposite poles, the two ultimates of male (yang) and female (yin), positive and negative, light and dark, and any similarly opposing poles you can come up with. These poles coexist in everything, and the stronger pole dominates and endows every individual thing with a dominant feature. But then, it all depends: an entity regarded as yin in one light can be regarded as yang in another light. A male, simply as a male, is yang, but as a son to a parent he is yin; then again, as a brother to a sister he is yang, but when this boy grows up and gets a job, as an employee he is yin.

While yin and yang are opposite poles, in the long run they are supposed to comple-ment each other. This is indicated in the *taeguk*, the yin-yang symbol of one circle formed by two commas nestling head to tail against each other. This principle is so basic to Koreans that we use the taeguk as the basic design in our national flag.

The movement of the universe depends on whether the opposites yin and yang oppose or complement each other. And here is where the Koreans' three-comma symbol comes in. Koreans see a third essential element, the realm of man, as an interposed factor which decides whether the two yin and yang poles oppose, thereby causing unbalance and distress, or cooperate and allow things to run smoothly.

In the myth which relates the origin of Korea's first king, the Son of Heaven visited Earth. Coincidentally, there was a female bear on Earth who wanted to become a human. Here we have the two essential realms of Heaven and Earth. This bear was eventually allowed to become a human. Then she and the Son of Heaven united, and out of this union came the first king of the Korean race. This myth expresses the inter-mediary role of the third element, the human realm (for the bear became a human), which formed a bridge between the two opposite poles, the realm of Heaven and the realm of Earth, thus making possible the formation of a nation.

So when a Korean farms his land he does it in terms of these three ultimate realms. For crops to grow Heaven must provide just the right amount of sun and rain. Too much sun causes drought, too much rain causes flooding. This follows the yin-yang princi-ple. But even if the climate is perfect it is useless without a third essential, land, to make use of it. Let us consider this in terms of a yin heaven and a yang earth; even with a perfect balance of these two the crops would amount to nothing more than a prairie or weed patch without man there to plow and weed. So this is the principle of the three essential realms. Man is the agent which synthesizes the powers of heaven and earth and crystallizes them into something productive–or destructive.

One scholar saw in the symbols of Chris-tianity (its cross) and Buddhism (the swasti-ka) a cartwheel illustrating the functioning of the universe. We might apply this perspi-cacious observation to the taeguk's universe. Compare the three cartwheels, though, and see which symbol would seem to roll most smoothly. And therewith acheive a better understanding of the meaning of the princi-ple of ultimate realms.

Nature's Own Pavilion
팔각정
Palkakjong

The Pentagon has more sides than the usual four. Whenever one hears the word pentagon the first thought that comes to mind is something like the savage atom bomb of World War II. That is because America's Department of Defense is housed there.

But when one sees or hears of Korea's most widely known architectural counterpart, the octagonal pavilion in Seoul's Kyongbok Palace, what comes to mind is just the opposite of war–a scene of nature as beautiful as an oriental landscape painting. This is because the octagonal pavilion is representative of the culture which created it.

Wherever you find a quiet river hamlet nestled at the foot of a lofty, craggy cliff, you will find the pavilion sitting there in its fortuitous spot commanding a scenic view of the river. In fact, one photographer who visited Korea tells of how, in his travels through the countryside, whenever he came upon a scene he considered worth photographing, there would be the inevitable pavilion.

The value of a pavilion is not in how nicely it is designed or how grand it is, but in where it is situated. Let's borrow that term in such common currency these days, "the ecology of architecture," to use in an example. It is not only beause the pavilion is a place to relax in nature that we regard place as more important than structure. From

long ago we have selected a site for a house only after we determine the quality of the site itself, and have therefore devoted much more concern to establishing the place for the house than we have for the house. Be it a royal palace in the capital city or a thatch-roof house in the deepest mountains, a Buddhist temple or a grave, the concept involved in establishing the sight has the status of religious doctrine or ideological principle. In fact, in the ancient *Heritage of Three Kingdoms* it tells of how, instead of going out and searching for a building site for a temple, they would build a temple wherever they found a beautifully situated piece of land. A good example of this is Sokullam, the magical site of the famous Buddha Grotto, with its gorgeous view of mountains, fields and sea in idyllic harmony.

The architecture of the octagonal pavilion is representative of that philosophy of architecture which minimizes the structure and maximizes its surroundings. Because of this there is in the pavilion a complete absence of the wall so essential to that structure-oriented architecture which delineates inside and outside. The ruling concept inherent in the octagonal pavilion is not one of eight walls but of eight individual open spaces. And so in each of these eight perspectives on nature you get a different view. Just like any painting has its frame, the pavilion pro-

vides frames of scenes from nature. Primal nature is enhanced into a work of art colonaded with eight pillars. It appears as if those who built the pavilion possessed a creative sense of camera angle long before the camera was ever thought of. The Japanese developed the art of garden landscaping and brought the beauty of nature into their yard. The Korean developed the art of pavilion landscaping by going out to nature's yard.

When we sit on the floor of the pavilion nature is both a folding screen and a garden. We sense then the inseparable relationship which exists between the pavilion and its surrounding nature. And we know that we are part of that relationship.

Tripitaka Koreana: The Sword Conquered
팔만대장경
Palmandaejangkyong

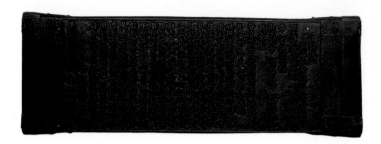

The Mongolian invasion of the two continents of Europe and Asia was even more sweeping and devastating than the great historical conquests of Alexander, Caesar and Napoleon. This is the basis for the passage in the legend which tells of how "the Mongolians left nothing behind them but dust."

It was because of the Mongolians' march through Korea that the Koreans were able to present the world with two remarkable feats. These miracles were accomplished not with the help of nature, such as the "heavenly wind" which the Japanese say propelled their kamikazes, but with their own human hands.

During the Mongolians' march through nation after nation, no matter how great the nation its leadership would go down on their knees almost as soon as the Mongolians crossed their border. In Korea, however, the Koryo dynasty (918-1392 A.D.) was able to put up a successful resistance of thirty years on the tiny island of Kanghwa. They resisted there so long, in fact, that a world map made in Europe at that time showed Korea as an island nation.

But the proud memory of a stubborn resistance is not the only remarkable consequence of the Mongolian invasion. Whereas the Mongolians left nothing but dust and ashes behind them in other nations, they

unwittingly left in Korea a tremendous cultural legacy. In 1231, the eighteenth year of Kojong, the invaders set fire to the nation's complete set of Buddhist sutras, kept at that time in Buin Temple. But the Koreans, even as they persevered in their resistance on Kanghwa, set about to carve the printing blocks for a new collection of the Buddhist classics. After sixteen years of adversity and deprivation, the nation managed to complete this stupendous project of eighty thousand printing blocks, the *Tripitaka Koreana*. Today these can be seen at Haein Temple, in the mountains near Taegu.

If one of rationalist thinking had heard of this at the time he would have asked why on earth they did not use the same resources it took for such a mind-boggling task to make a few more weapons. Why, he would have asked, dissipate the nation's strength trying to stand up to such a ferocious enemy with some superstitious Buddha-power? But if these people of Koryo times had tried to resist the Mongolian military power with their own military power, they never would have resisted long enough to even make it onto Kanghwa. They had to fight the Mongolians with a power the Mongolians did not have.

Thanks to the devotion and persistence they used in managing to carve that staggering number of printing blocks for the sutras, they were able to record in the annals of history their feat of resistance against the Mongolian hordes. Because they armed themselves with the sutra printing blocks against the Mongolian soldiers and weaponry, the Mongolians, despite their might, were not able to reduce Korea to a pile of ashes as they had other nations.

Using the same spirit and culture and technology needed to carve those eighty thousand *Tripitaka Koreana* blocks, Korea became the first country to develop metal type. Then, a half century before Gutenberg invented copper type in 1440, Koreans were already printing books with it.

In the end we can say for the much maligned Mongolians that they left a lot more in Korea than dust and desolation. Whatever their motivations, they laid the foundation for the world's first printing culture.

The Wind Bell: Where Fish Swim the Sky

풍경
Pungkyong

We can get a glimpse of authentic American sentiment in the occasional appearance of the music box in the cowboy movie. The music box is lying there on the ground next to a smoldering covered wagon or log cabin. The lonely cowboy hero stoops down, picks it up, puts it to his ear, and is overwhelmed by poignant memories.

An analysis of the meaning in that sound produced by the music box will tell us of the nature of that culture. It is a culture of automation, established patterns of repetitive sound, the momentariness of sound stopped in time. This culture likes gadgets which reflect the practicality of mundane life, which we see in artifacts like the cosmetics case that plays music when you open its lid. All these elements incorporate the nature of the sound produced by the music box, and point directly to the cultural inclinations of the West.

If we were to suggest something in Korea which arouses emotions corresponding to those the music box arouses in the cowboy, it would have to be the wind bell. But the wind bell manifests to us something diametrically opposed to the music box. For one thing, the wind bell's counterpart to the man-made mechanical quality of the music box is the heaven-sent wind of nature. The wind bell does not have that mechanism which hides inside the music box. The wind bell produces its sound not with the force provided by a spring but that of the wind. That is why the wind bell is not used inside a house or in a box, where there is no movement of the air, but is hung outside from the corner of the roof.

Another difference is in the repetitive song produced by the music box. The music box is often used as a stage prop in scenes of reminiscence because the familiar melody produces a conditioned response. The sound of the wind bell is a monotone, but because its amplitude and the pitch of the notes emanating from it depend on the strength of the wind, there is no redundant pattern. It gives an effect not of repetition but of sequential individual events, since no two winds blow the same.

The third difference is that the wind bell does not have to be wound. Whenever the wind blows it rings, unlike the music box, which grinds to a stop when its spring winds down.

Finally, the wind bell would never be considered an article of practical use. Its distinguishing feature is that it has nothing to do with the reality of everyday life. A flat metal fish for catching the wind hangs down from the wind bell's clapper. Here is a fish which normally swims under water, now working its fins in the blue sky. As long as we have our eyes on it we are in a surrealistic reverie. Another unusual thing about this fish is that fish do not sing, like birds do. But this fish swimming in the air sings, like a goldfinch.

So the place where the wind bell is ringing takes on the hues of the blue water of the Dragon King's water palace. It is a place where fish and birds break the boundaries of wind and wave in their sojourn by the eave of the roof. This is the cultural inclination of the Korean, the image and sound of his feelings.

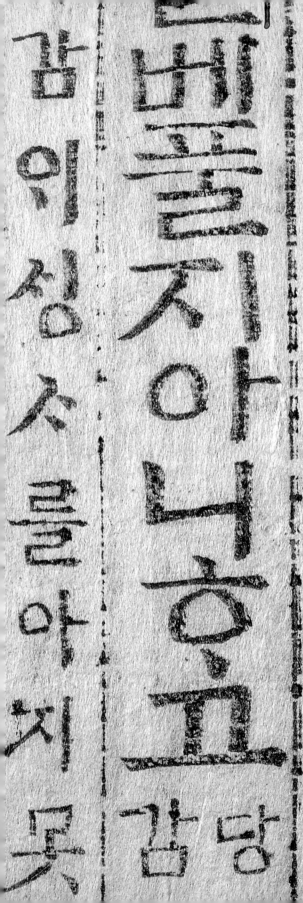

Principles of Hangul Script

한글

Hangul

Both the Koreans and the Japanese have for centuries been part of the magnificent Chinese cultural realm, and while their grammar is basically different from Chinese, have used the Chinese writing system. At the same time they are also very proud of their own indigenous systems of writing, which they established after having for so long relied solely on the Chinese system.

It should be noted, though, that the two nations' phonetic alphabets, while they originated from the Chinese writing system, are each a product of different processes of development. Japan's hiragana and katagana scripts both retain the basic form of the ideographic characters in the Chinese system. For example, the Japanese letter ア is based on the Chinese character 阿, both of which are pronounced the same in Japanese. And the letter あ is an abbreviated form of the Chinese character 安 in its cursive form. In some cases, the character is almost identical to its Chinese prototype: the Japanese イ is a very obvious abbreviation of the Chinese character 尹, which is actually an abbreviation of the basic character 伊.

Many Korean words, along with their pronunciation, originated in Chinese words. But *hangul*, which literally means Korean script, is a product of a system completely different from Chinese characters. One might think that because Korea transmitted the Chinese writing system to Japan its indigenous writing system would resemble the Chinese more than the Japanese system would. But there is no imitation of Chinese characters in the Korean system. Hangul letters are purely phonetic representations, the original creation of Korean court scholars. Each character is a one-syllable sound which is represented in a unit comprised of from one to four letters.

Hangul is different from the Chinese in another way, too. One distinguishing feature of the unique characters of the Korean system is that if you change the position of the character, maybe turn it on its side or invert it, there is a basic difference in the pronunciation of the character. This does not happen in the Chinese ideogram—even if we were to take one of the lines in a Chinese character, or the whole character itself, and face it in another direction, there would be no confusing the sound of one character with another character. It would simply look wrong. The same goes for English, except for the *m*, which, turned on its head, is a *w*. In hangul, the vertical or horizontal direction and top, bottom, inside or outside placement of even only one line will often change the pronunciation of that character.

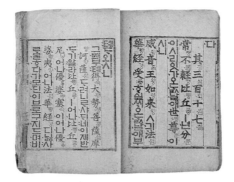

If a character is comprised of only one vowel (with no consonant) a circle is its basis, and to the circle's top, bottom or one of its sides there is a structure of two perpendicular lines in the form of a short-legged T; the position of this T–upright, inverted, or on its side with its leg facing either inside or outside–determines the pronunciation of the vowel. This T element by itself would be meaningless if it were removed from the positional and directional context of the circle it centers on.

The significance of one line's relative position and direction applies not only to vowels. The linear elements comprising the consonant, too, have meaning only in relation to each other. If you were to turn the character for word (문, a consonant-vowel-consonant combination) on its head, you would find yourself with the character for the word bear (곰).

Hangul, like the phonology of the Korean language, is structured in accordance with the correspondence and opposition which coexist between two poles. In linguistic terminology, its elements in relation to each other are more emic (distinctive) than etic (non-distinctive). Note the opposite direction of the T in these vowel sets: the counterpart of 오 (as in hope) is 우 (as in flute),

and that of 어 (as in fought) is 아 (as in father). Every letter identifies itself in relation to its distinctiveness from other letters.

The structure and pronunciation of all the consonants are based on the directional and positional composition of the consonant letters ㄱ (pronounced between k and g) and ㄴ (n). The consonants might be regarded as derivatives of these two basic letters, as is evident in their forms: ㄷ ㄹ ㅁ ㅂ.

The structures of these letters did not just happen out of the blue. There is principle behind them. When the T is turned on its side like this ㅏ, the long vertical line represents Heaven, and the horizontal cross line when the T is upright, like this ㅗ, represents Earth. The shorter leg of the T in this position represents mankind. The universe was created in the image of its creator, and hangul letters illustrate the system of this universe.

The form of the letter also represents the position and shape of the tongue in its formation of the letter's corresponding sound. Look at the ㄹ, and you can easily imagine the tongue forming the flapped r. Another good example of the letter form's representation of its sound is the aspiration marks on some of the consonants–you can tell without even knowing the alphabet that they are there to indicate stress. The aspirated ㄱ,

for example, is ㅋ; aspirated ㄷ is ㅌ.

Hangul manifests the structuralism inherent in the way Koreans do and make things. The variants of affixation and cancellation, which give hangul its fecundity, together with the elements of abstractness and spatiality, make hangul a universe in symbols.

Oriental Medicine: Healing Through Words

한약
Hanyak

In both Korean and English 'discomfort' is the origin of some words for illness. So when we treat an illness, besides the body we must also attend to the psyche. Treating only the body is not real treatment; that would be more like fixing a car or overhauling a robot.

Western medicine is advanced in technology, but in providing care to the psyche it lags far behind. Take, for instance, the treatment of a child. It is one irony of modern civilization that when a child is sick it suffers more anguish from fear of the treatment than it does from the sickness itself. The child fears the treatment so much, in fact, that when it is petulant, instead of "The policeman's going to come and take you to jail," the threat is now, "The doctor's going to come and give you a shot." The doctor with his needle is more fearsome than the policeman with his gun. This shows how distant the relationship is between the doctor and his patient.

The doctor's demeanor is not the only problem. That hospital atmosphere of sterile rationalism—everything white, everything Stainless steel—lacks any touch of human feeling. Even the names of medication have no more personality than, and are just as sterile as the names of the chemical elements which comprise them. And look at the names western medicine gives to its

nutritional supplements, names that sound as matter-of-fact as the chemistry lab in which they originated. Vitamin A, Vitamin B...these names are all no more than letters and numbers, with no character to them whatsoever.

In oriental medicine the supplement's name tells what it is supposed to accomplish. The one which enhances the conjugal relationship, for example, is called "Mutual Harmony Potion." And there is that potion for general vigor and virility, whose name announces "ten ingredients to get the whole body in shape." These names have character because they reflect the nature of the ingredients that go into the medicine which they identify, and these ingredients are natural herbs, not synthetic chemicals.

If you ask the western doctor whether the medication he has prescribed will cure you, eight times out of ten he will say, "Well, we'll just have to wait and see." But almost any doctor of oriental medicine will answer what the patient needs to hear: "Just one tablet and you'll be as good as new." And why not? The very sound of the name of a herbal medication makes the patient feel better as soon as he hears it.

In Western medicine, then, the patient is treated with technology, whereas in oriental medicine the patient is treated with heart. The former offers the patient cold facts,

while the latter extends to the patient that last ray of hope he needs so desperately. This is evident in each doctor's bedside manner. The western doctor is pure intellect, and you can see this in that hard, intense look in his eyes as he scrutinizes the message from his stethoscope; the herbal doctor is pure spirit, his eyes half closed in meditation on the warm pulse.

We can best understand the efficacy of oriental herbal medicine by considering how it is prepared. The thick white ceramic bowl which the doctor uses to combine his herbs resembles the heavy mixing bowl Granny used in her kitchen more than it does any silver scalpel. And the name of the medication which the doctor writes on the medication's package is in exotic Chinese characters, bringing to mind some mystic's charm.

Another absolutely essential element in the preparation of medicine is devotion. Herbal medicine is not administered by the doctor directly to the patient, it is administered by the patient's mother or wife. It is she that brews it back at home, watching it simmer for hours till it is just right. It is she that sees to it that the patient gets it at just the right time, whatever the hour of night or day.

Outside on a winter day the fields are covered white and a cold wind sweeps across them. I cough, shiver with a chill down to

my bones. And what comes to mind is that heavy white mixing bowl, those mystical hieroglyphics of the medication's name written in cursive Chinese script. And I feel the warm presence of mother serving that medication with the aromatic fragrance of its herbs.

In the misty steam wafting from the brewing medication and in herbal medicine's language of comfort I find reconciliation with life.

The Earthenware Vessel
항아리
Hangari

It is said that the beauty of sculpture comes from its embodiment of material substantiality. In a portrait you can see and spiritually sense the object's form, but in sculpture you can actually feel it with your hands. R. Hamann says that in terms of physics, matter means substance, the opposite of vacuum; inherent in it is a resistance which prevents penetration. Therefore, the harder something is, the stronger is its feature of substance. That is the reason sculptors will use granite when they can.

For something to have true substantiality it must have true form. A material may be hard, but if it has no definite form it is difficult to regard it as a substance. The wall, for instance, with its hard but undefined surface, does not give that sense of having true substance. The more convexity or concavity an object has, the closer it comes to the definition of having substance. Having said this, we must also note that if the object's surface is too irregular its feature of substantiality weakens. It must be a concrete object, simple and definite in form, for us to say it manifests true substance.

This relates not only to the aspect of form; tonally, too, for an object to have true substance it must be opaque and look impermeable. So it is that they say the more achromatic an object is, the more pronounced its substantiality. According to this, then, a material of bright colors or one which gives a sense of transparency is not suitable for sculpture. If we apply these classical principles of sculptural art to Korea's earthenware vessel we can see why this household item has received universal recognition as

an objet d' art.

Korea's earthenware vessels incorporate all the basic elements of sculpture mentioned above. First, though this vessel is made of earth, because it has been fired to give it a surface as hard as a gem it has great solidity. Its rotundity enhances its solidity. Its surface is smooth and tight as human skin and its tones are restrained, thus giving it the opacity which is essential to substantiality.

The earthenware vessel, because of its features of solidity, rotundity, smoothness and achromatic tones, embodies the essential properties of substantiality and is therefore archetypal sculptural art. When we see the hard solidity of this vessel we feel an utter tranquility which the soft, warm human body cannot achieve. In the museum those signs ask us, "Do not touch" the sculptures and pottery, but it is very difficult to restrain ourselves from touching a sculpture as alive as the earthenware vessel.

While this vessel has true substantiality it also incorporates a true vacuum. Its form gives a sense of fullness, but this comes from its empty inside. This property of emptiness is, of course, the opposite of substantiality.

That solid but simultaneously vacuous form reminds us of the poignant fragility of the human body. No matter how flawless an earthenware vessel may be, one senses in it the potentiality of breakage. Its fate from the time it is made is to break. Each of these vessels which comes out of the kiln is one more sad, vulnerable body engendered by the womb of fire.

Tiger: Laughter in Brute Force

호랑이
Horangi

"Tiger, Tiger burning bright..." Blake's tiger is a fierce beast which symbolizes power and conquest. Koreans, though, look on the tiger as friendly Hodori, the Seoul Olympics mascot. It is no coincidence that he was selected as mascot, for he is a Korean tradition. In ordinary circumstances he might be a ferocious man-eating beast, but once he becomes part of the Korean cultural environment he forgets all about his sharp teeth and claws and turns into as lovable and sweet a thing as a country grandpa.

In the ancient annals *Heritage of Three Kingdoms* the tiger, far from being something which would harm people, is portrayed as the model of selflessness, who would even offer his own life for his human compatriot. And in one classical story the tiger appears as a creature with wit and wisdom, who berates and then enlightens a corrupted Confucian scholar.

You can see even better how he has metamorphosed in the Korean imagination if you take a close look at how he is portrayed in folk paintings. Many remark that they feel more amused than awed when they see him in such a context. Look at his posture, look at his expression. No matter where you look you will find nothing of aggressiveness. If you happened upon this character on a mountain path, rather than wanting to flee for your life you would feel like asking him for a light and then sitting down for a pleasant chat over a cigarette. In fact, in one folk painting there is that wonderful scene of old Tiger holding the long pipe in his teeth with his friend Rabbit lighting it for him.

In some other folk paintings he has another partner, Magpie. There are many interpretations for this, but the one thing we can be sure of is that in this kind of folk painting we have an illustration of the cosmological relationships which make up our universe; the tiger symbolizes Earth and the magpie symbolizes Heaven. And the pine tree there between the tiger and the magpie serves as an intermediary in this relationship.

In fact, in indigenous religions the tiger, as a deity of nature, is guardian of Earth. But he is not the stern patriarchal type of guardian that one might expect of a beast who can in other circumstances be quite ferocious. He is closer to the earth-mother, who gives birth and enfolds the child in affectionate embrace.

In Korea we have had many powerful tyrants and not a few autocrats in positions of authority. Those who lacked the character of the tiger in our folk paintings never lasted long. A leader like Hitler could never emerge from a land which hosts the culture of the tiger.

Traditional Koreans would never think of imprisoning the tiger inside a fence. In their imagination, in their folk paintings, he is a friend. In such a culture adversity and violence turn into laughter. It is like the humor we see in the *Legend of Hungbu*, when his cruel sister-in-law smacks the starving Hungbu in the mouth with the rice ladle. Does Hungbu get angry, or despair? On the contrary, he takes the kernels sticking to his cheek and gratefully gobbles them down.

The Brazier: A Crypt for Fire

화로
Hwaro

There are two kinds of fire. One exists in the form of flame, and the other exists in the form of the ember. And the instruments which help man to use fire for his purposes can be divided into two categories. One is for lighting a flame and keeping that flame burning, and the other is for holding and preserving the fire inside charcoal.

The potbellied stove of the West is for making a fire of flame. So its form is based on its stoking chamber and chimney. The fan and the poker are used for combustion and increasing the intensity of the fire inside the stove.

The brazier is different from the stove in that it is for holding and preserving fire in its other form. This kind of fire is an older fire than the one made in the stove, since it has already passed through the stage of flame. To express the difference between the two heating devices in extreme terms, the potbellied stove is there at the birth of a fire, and the brazier is there at its death. So the brazier is not designed in accordance with the nature of flame but is based on the fundamentals of potential ash, which would mean that it is a rather paradoxical stove. Because of this the brazier has no need of any such thing as a stoking chamber or a chimney. It is for the death of a flame, an urn for its ashes.

While it is true that braziers come in all different shapes and sizes, they all share two points in common. They have that same basic form of a vessel for holding heat, and they serve as the grave of the fire. So when we use the brazier for heating, the stick which we use is for tamping down, to smother and bury the charcoal so it does not burn too fast. This is quite different from the potbellied stove's poker, which is used to stir the wood and provide more oxygen for the fire to make it burn hotter.

The brazier ultimately functions to cool its fire. "When the embers cool in the clay brazier, the night wind in the field sounds like galloping horses." The beauty of the brazier is not in a raging flame but in its dying embers. This is a beauty of the old, not the new. In the words of the Korean poet Mi-dang, we appreciate the brazier not as we would the spring gossamer but as we would the first frost of autumn, not the peach blossom but the chrysanthemum, not the quick song of the swallow nor the sharp talons of the hawk but the slow thousand-year flight of the crane.

That is why the brazier is best at grandmother's side or in grandfather's room. Grandma's stories were always their most pleasant when we heard them by the brazier, and you never saw Grandpa look more peaceful than when he was sleeping right there next to it.

Foreigners, who are used to seeing beauty only in youth, are surprised when they see Korea's elderly. They sense in these elderly a beauty they cannot quite put their finger on, something of the dignified, stately countenance of a Taoist immortal. In spite of having lived a difficult life these elderly show nothing of the sallow, twisted, shrunken decrepitude of the elderly in the city's old people's homes. The charm of our elderly originates in this culture which knows the aesthetics of the ash.

This culture is not one of the consuming flame. It is one in which the waning ember, having done its task in the kitchen, is transferred to the brazier to be kept for its final moments. This culture is one of preservation rather than of consumption.

Appendix

A-Frame

지게 Jige

The *jige*, which Koreans use to transport things, is made of two long wood poles, each with a prong sticking out back to bear the load. These two poles are connected by four crossbars of either metal or wood; they are wider apart at the bottom than at the bead, so that the *jige* can stand upright, with the support of another pole attached to the center of the top crossbar. Where the *jige* rests on the back of the carrier there is a mat woven from straw. There are two shoulder straps, attached to each pole at the second crossbar from the top and at the bottom of the pole, much like a modern backpack. An indication of the enduring utility of the *jige*'s design is the fact that the general design of the modern backpack is basically the same, and the *jige* is still used very much in construction work in the city and all sorts of work in the countryside, generally wherever and whenever there is a heavy load to carry.

Bell

종 Jong

The sophisticated aesthetic features of Korea's traditional bell are very closely linked with the spread of Buddhism. After Buddhism was transmitted to Korea from India (through China) it spread its roots deep and wide among Korea's general populace. It naturally followed that many temple bells were produced, and with this came a creative development in style.

When we speak of the Korean bell we have in mind the Buddhist temple bell. Its basic function, of course, is to mark the time of day, but along with this it serves a religious function. It is used on the eve of the new year to ring out the old and ring in the new; involved in this practice was the expurgation of the 108 passions (and their 108 troublesome consequences). The bell is also rung 108 times every morning, for this same purpose.

In the sound of that temple bell we are reminded of the transiency of all things in life, and that through the Buddha we can be saved from our passions and vices. So the bell indicates to us both the philosophical and the religious nature of Buddhism and raises us to a state of piety and devotion.

Korea's temple bell has secured a firm reputation as one of the world's best-crafted bells with its sophisticated appearance and technically advanced casting methods.

Booty

버선 Boson

Over the centuries of its existence the booty, worn by male and female alike, has been referred to in literature under several terms. The word used these days—*boson*—is a slight modification of *boshon*, which we find mentioned in a document from 1527.

Today's stylish, comfortable booty has evolved gradually from the original purely functional one used only to protect the feet. The toe now curves elegantly up to a point. The ankle is a snug fit but there is more room at the top, for the foot to enter easily. There is a seam on each booty running diagonally from the big toe back to the outer edge of the heel, which indicates which foot the booty goes on.

These days, because socks are worn with the increasingly popular western clothing, the booty is not as commonly used as it was in the past. When one does wear the traditional clothing, though, tasteful style dictates use of the booty.

The Brazier

화로 Hwaro

The brazier is used in many ways, but it is used mainly to heat a cold room in the winter and to keep alive the embers for later use.

When a Korean thinks of old Korea what invariably comes to mind is the brazier, since it was such an integral part of everyday life. The Korean will think of village life when he thinks of traditional Korea, and there was nothing as indispensable and beloved in village life as the brazier.

There was no restriction as to where the brazier could be used. In the kitchen, the female's quarters, the living room, the male's quarters, the entrance hallway, the courtyard . . . anywhere people went the brazier went. In the countryside the brazier was either of cast iron or earthenware, but usually of earthenware. Somewhat more sophisticated braziers are made of brass or stone; these are usually found in the cities or wealthier homes in the countryside. The distinctive features of stone braziers, as opposed to iron ones, are their capacity to hold heat longer and the greater diversity in their designs.

Coin
엽전 Yopjon

The Korean coin was round and flat like coins elsewhere, but with a square hole in its center.

The Chinese first casted this type of coin in the third century B.C., when the Ch'in dynasty unified the whole country under its realm. This coin retained its basic design up to the Ch'ing dynasty (1610-1904). It was introduced to Korea from T'ang China in 621, and a coin with the same design was first minted in Korea in 996.

Condiments Bay
장독대 Changdokdae

This is an absolute essential in any traditional Korean home. It is generally located in an eastern corner of the yard, where it can get lots of sun. If the yard is spacious the condiments bay is found in the backyard. If the house does not have much of a backyard, what yard there is will be in front, and this is where you will find the condiments bay.

A wife's reputation in housekeeping skills used to be determined by the state of her condiments bay, so she devoted a lot of effort to keeping it clean and tidy. The condiments bay is a good indication of how much importance Koreans place in the processing and preservation of their condiments.

Earthenware Vessel
항아리 Hangari

Earthenware jars have been in use in many areas of the world for a long, long time, but it was not until the technique of pottery-making was developed that we had anything more than the simple bowl with dark brown glaze. The first earthenware was made in the neolithic age, when humans learned agriculture and settled in one place and stopped wandering for their food; this was unglazed clayware. Primitive as it was, we use the same principle in making the more sophisticated glazed pottery of today.

Floor Cushions and Mat
방석 Bangsok

When we think of the floor cushion what usually comes to mind is a square pad like a flat, tightly bound sack, stuffed with cotton and covered with silk, cotton, or some synthetic fabric. This one is usually used in the winter.

There are others, though, without stuffing, which are used in the summer. These are more pad than cushion. One kind is woven from the carefully selected soft, gray inner fiber of the sedge plant stalk.

There is also the larger mat, enough for several people to use together. It is made of the skin of the sedge's stalk. It can be round or square, but usually has a colorful pattern of flower and bird in its center. Each juncture of warp and woof is colored to give a general effect of embroidery.

Another kind of mat is woven from wheat straw. This one is quite thick and is mainly for use outside.

Floor Table
상 Sang

While most traditional floor tables have four legs there have been some with three, two, and even one. Any sort of intricate design might be carved in the frieze, an essential element in the whole design. Tables are named for their design, the

region where they were made, or the wood they are made of.

It is not known when the table was first used in Korea, but tables do appear in paintings on the walls of ancient tombs from the Koguryo and Shilla dynasties. Today we have many exquisitely crafted tables from the latter half of the Chosun dynasty. The oldest table preserved from our past is about two hundred years old. Antiques are highly valued these days, and these floor tables can be found in an honored place in many homes and museums.

Folding Screen
병풍 Byongpung

The folding screen serves the dual purpose of utility and art. It was originally used to block drafts in the room, but later came to be used to display paintings, calligraphy, and embroidery illustrations as well; in modern times it is used mainly for artistic purposes and interior decoration. The folding screen has been in use for almost 2,000 years, since Han China, but its use became widespread around the seventh century A.D., in T'ang China. There is a record of it having been exported from Korea, along with precious metals and silk, to Japan in the late seventh century, and it is frequently mentioned in Koryo dynasty (tenth to thirteenth centuries) literature. We have no folding screens from the early Chosun dynasty of the fifteenth century, but have many from the dynasty's remaining years.

The usual folding screen has eight, ten, or twelve panels. Screens with four or six panels, though, are not that unusual, and there is even one low, wide type of two panels. We also have a screen specially designed for protecting the head of the person sleeping on the floor mat from night drafts. There are screens with one art theme and screens with several themes, screens with rubbings, seal stampings, and several others of varied functions and designs.

The theme of the folding screen which served as the background of the king's throne, instead of the usual landscape or orchid, was the sun and moon together with the Ten Immortals embroidered in it. In some folding screens of this sort the sun and moon are formed from bronze.

Gourd
박 Bak

The gourd originated in India and Africa, and still grows wild there. The vegetable was first cultivated in China 2,000 years ago; it is thought that China introduced it to Korea.

The role of the gourd in the legend of Hungbu is interesting, in that Hungbu's gourd recalls the term "gourd of plenty" which appears in western writing and speech. Hungbu, the ill-treated but right-minded younger brother of wicked Nolbu, was rewarded for his goodness and industry by the treasures delivered in gourds, whose seeds were delivered by a bird Hungbu had nursed from a broken leg.

Hungbu worked very bard to help his wife and children after his elder brother kicked them all off the family estate. As Hungbu worked, Nolbu enjoyed himself. Maybe there is a related lesson in the fact that the gourd blossom opens late in the day and closes early the next morning. The gourd of plenty may be accessible to only the very industrious among us.

Graves
무덤 Mudom

Korea has several kinds of graves, and each has its own name. One name designates a mound with trees around it, another a grave covered by a structure, and there are a few others. In recent years, however, though the vocabulary remains, it is only the grave for royalty for which a special term is used. Now. for most people, a grave is a grave.

Burial rites in Korea are generally Confucian, with some indigenous shamanist trappings. Long after burial, the grave is visited annually for the Confucian memorial rites, and it may also be visited again by a shaman. If things are not going well with the descendants of the spirit of the deceased, either a shaman or even a Confucian may decide it is because the spot for the grave was selected in violation of the principles of geomancy, or was moved after burial from a good location to one unacceptable to the grave's occupant. In such a case, the shaman may take the living members there to perform rites for the placation of the occupant's spirit. The geomancer will recommend moving the grave elsewhere.

Hairpin
비녀 Binyo

There is reference to the ornamental hairpin in *Heritage of Three Kingdoms*, the annals of the Three Kingdoms period (first to seventh centuries). In writings from the eighteenth century we can see that a great variety of pins must have developed in that century. This may be due to the fact that in the eighteenth century females were prohibited from displaying their feminine charms, and so had to put their hair up in a bun. Because the hairpin was used by all Korean women it naturally developed into an element of fashion, despite sanctions against such display, and it took on the role of personal accessory. Distinction between the high and low classes was quite severe in the Chosun dynasty, and the hairpin reflected this distinction. Women of the aristocracy wore pins made of gold and silver and gems, commonly jade, while women of other classes wore pins fashioned from such materials as wood, horn, and bone.

Hand Fan
부채 Buchae

The paper or the fabric webbing of the fan is applied to thin slats of bamboo. Korea's best hand fans are made in the southwestern provinces of North and South Cholla.

Like so many instruments of daily use the fan originated with a functional purpose but soon awoke to its potential in serving ceremonial and social functions. At traditional weddings, for instance, both the bride and groom hide their faces with a fan.

The hand fan is also a much appreciated accomplice in art. Painters, calligraphers and literati adorn fans with artwork and poetry. A painting or calligraphy is often drawn on fan paper, and then the work is mounted on a scroll. This scroll, without the addition of handle or slats, is then displayed on the wall. Some of Korea's best classical art appears in this manner.

There is even a classical dance in which the fan is the theme; in fact, the "fan dance" gets its name from its main character. And the sorceress considers the fan an essential in the performance of shaman rites, in which dance is an integral part.

One fan which has maintained a functional purpose is the long-handled one used in the home to swat mosquitoes and get the iron's coals red hot. There is another kind, this one circular, which is used to shield oneself from the heat of the sun.

Hangul
한글 Hangul

The official term for this system of twenty-eight characters created by King Se-jong (r. 1419-1450) was something like "Phonetic System for Enlightenment of the People." Somewhat less official terms were "Korean writing," "national script," "a systematic table of Korean sounds" and "the language in written form," and less kindly, "hieroglyphics" (stressing the strange form of the system's characters), "script for children," "a system of useless knowledge," and "script for illiterates." The last three terms originated from the Confucian tradition that the only script worthy of a gentleman was Chinese characters, and the fact that the new Korean script was much easier to learn than Chinese characters (a learned man would know around ten thousand characters). The Korean script therefore, deserved only the attention of women, children, and those who otherwise could learn no system of writing.

The term *hangul* became widely used before the script itself became popular. After being used a while it gave way to the term "national language" in the process of the country's modernization and the awakening of a consciousness of Korea as a nation. Recently, though the nationalistic consciousness remains intact, the script is again being referred to popularly as *hangul*, with the term "national language" being used now to refer to the entire language (including the country's literature). The term *hangul* was popularized mainly through the efforts of Ju Shi-kyong (1876-1914), Korea's pioneer in linguistics, who turned study of both the language and its script into an academic discipline. It is largely through his efforts that *hangul* is now almost completely standardized.

Ink Brush

붓 But

The bristle of the common ink brush usually comes from the hair of the racoon, but the hairs of the rabbit, sheep, deer, weasel, horse, cat and roe are often also used. Thus the bristles of our brushes range from the very soft and pliant to the very stiff and firm, from long to stubby, depending on the brush's intended use. In the old days rat whiskers, the feathers of the chicken, and even the hair of infants were used as bristle.

Besides the bristle brush there are other instruments used for producing special artistic effects. Heads are made from one of a number of natural materials, including bamboo, arrowroot, and dry wood.

Kat: Traditional Headgear

갓 Kat

The *kat* originated as a protection against sun and rain and evolved into a symbol of noble rank. It was originally of two general categories. There was the straw *bangnip*, which resembled a very broad overturned straw bowl and was worn often for work and travel; then there was the *pyongyangja*, a conical object rounded off at the top, with a brim a few inches wide. The headgear came to be used to show noble rank in the Three Kingdoms period (first to seventh centuries). Over the centuries, the *kat's* ornamentation and the method of making it diverged into the many different *kats* worn during the Chosun Dynasty. The *kat* with which we are so familiar these days is the black horsehair *huknip*. This representative of Confucianism and the Chosun Dynasty is the latest development of all these different forms.

So, in a broad sense, all the various forms of the bangnip and the Pyongryang are called *kat*, but when we speak of the *kat* these days we are generally referring to the black horsehair headgear.

Kite

연 Yon

Kite flying is popular throughout the world, but especially in the countries of the Far East. And in any country of the Far East there is a great variety of kites, referred to in many different conceptual terms.

The records show that the kite was actually first used in Greece around 400 B.C. The Chinese Han Shin is recorded as having flown a kite around 200 B.C., for military purposes. There is also record of a Korean general who used a kite eight hundred years after the one documented in China. *Heritage of Three Kingdoms* tells of the Shilla dynasty general Kim Yu-shin who, in 646 A.D., to keep the people from panicking during a military crisis, sent up a burning kite at night and told them it was a fortuitous sign from heaven.

These days kites are flown for both fun and religious purposes. The object of the "kite fight" is to cross the string of the opponent's kite with your own and, by maneuvering the kite with both vigor and cunning dexterity, cause enough friction to cut the string of the opponent's kite and set it free. Grand competitions are held annually. The kite is used also to get rid of evil spirits. On the fifteenth day of the first month of the lunar calendar a kite inscribed with the Chinese character meaning "ward off evil spirits" is set flying and then frees itself and flies off when the ember that has been tied to its string burns through.

Knife

칼 Kal

Cutting edges can be categorized as anything between dagger and sword, according to their size, or anything between utensil and weapon, depending on how they are used. Development of the cutting edge began with the development of what we know as human intelligence; before man's intelligence really began to develop, the best cutting edge he had was the sharp edge or point of a rock or a piece of bone. It was only much later than this that man's discovery of copper-smelting gave him his first copper knife. Later came the bronze knife, and then the steel knife.

The Korean language has some expressions based on the knife or sword which have corresponding expressions in English. A variation on a metaphor from English, "like slicing water with a knife," is used to describe a relationship between two who have had a fight, but the relationship is so strong that it will mend as soon as the fight is over. Another expression, "like putting a sword into the hand of a child," is self-explanatory.

Komungo

거문고 Komungo

This representative string instrument of Korea is also referred to as the *hyonkum*. Sound is produced by plucking six silk strings strung over the sound box with a long bamboo plectrum. Because of its solemn and dignified sound it has always been venerated by the scholar steeped in learning and virtue. Even today we can hear its poignant strains accompanying both old favorites and those songs with lyrics from the classical poetry called *sijo*.

According to *Heritage of Three Kingdoms*, an

instrument of seven strings was sent over from Chin China in the sixth century A.D. The musician Wang San-ak, retaining the original form, modified its structure. (It is said that when he played the new instrument a black crane descended from the heavens and danced to the music's strains.)

On the wall of a burial mound from the Koguryo dynasty (first to seventh centuries), however, there is a painting with a *komungo* of the same basic form as the one we have today. This drawing was painted previous to Chin China. Thus there is the view that Korea already had the *komungo*, and that it may have spread to other countries during the Unified Shilla period (seventh to tenth centuries).

Lantern
초롱 Chorong

The ribs of the lantern are either bamboo slats or thin metal strips, and the shade protecting the candle inside is either colored paper or silk gauze, usually red and green. In the old days there was a great variety of these lanterns, the specific form and color of each depending on how this versatile utensil was used. It can be placed near the ground to light a road or path. or hung anywhere, from the hip of the roof, at the main gate, in the vestibule, and occasionally even in the kitchen. This lantern can also be carried easily, since it is so light and the candle is well protected from the wind. It was truly a friend to be out with at night.

Macrame
매듭 Maedup

In making the traditional macrame, silk is woven into twine, then the twine is died, and then two strings of twine are braided into the macrame's final form. Some macrame artisans begin with the tassel as the base and work out from this. However it is made, in the past macrame served as ornamentation in any number of ways, from a

pendant on the traditional Korean clothing to the trimmings on a sedan chair.

Humans began their civilization with the discovery of fire; then they progressed to the use of copper and iron, and went from there on to writing. To these basic steps in the march of humanity towards full civilization must be added the basic skill involved in the craft of macrame. It was the tying of knots that made possible hunting, the construction of dwellings, the transportation of goods, and the other essentials of civilization. This basic skill was the basis for the development of recording, marking, writing and design, and allowed us to move up from the primitive and intermediate stages of civilization to the more advanced stages.

Macrame is the offspring of that skill which enabled man to build his civilization into what it is now.

Mats
돗자리 Dotjari

The most popular mat in Korea is woven of the split stalks of sedge or candle rush. There are several other kinds of straw mat, made from rice straw, wheat straw and others, and in varying qualities of texture, from very fine to coarse. Whatever the material or texture of the mat, on a summer's evening in the countryside we can still see people lounging on it around a friendly fire out in the yard.

Kanghwa Island, off the west coast just a couple hours drive from Seoul, is regarded as the producer of the finest quality mats. The sedge which grows there is of a higher quality than elsewhere. So it is natural that Kanghwa's mat craftsmen have developed the craft to an art form.

They make two kinds of mats on Kanghwa. One is made from practically any kind of straw that can be used in a mat. The straw is hung from a horizontal pole at the top of a frame; each string is weighted at the bottom end with a stone. At the top, a piece of straw is laced horizontally

through the perpendicular strands and a knot is tied at every juncture with a perpendicular strand. This is the coarser kind, both because the straw is usually not sedge, and because of the knots. The other kind is finer. Sedge is always used, and the sedge strands are tightly woven, not knotted.

Millstone
맷돌 Maetdol

One roughly hewn stone, round, broad and flat. is placed on another similar stone; the bottom stone and top stone are connected with an axle impaled in the male bottom stone. The male remains stationary as the female is turned, clockwise, on the axle. Grain is placed in a hole at the top, the same hole which holds the axle; the grain falls between the stones and is ground there. The whole apparatus is centered in a depression in the ground, which functions as a basin to catch the millstone's production.

When two people work at this together one pours in the grain, but the two of them turn the top stone together. So they must both breathe in harmony to work in harmony, to keep the stone moving steadily; this makes the job easier, and produces a finer flour.

In one locale in Kangwon Province (on the east coast) they use a wood grinder which, like the stone grinder, has a thick, heavy plate both top and bottom. But on the surfaces which face each other are carved inter-fitting grooves.

On Cheju Island they have one grinding stone for producing rice flour. (This flour water is added to produce the sticky substance which is used in smoothing the wrinkles out of silk and ramie clothing after washing. The substance is applied to the clothes, and then the clothes are beaten with the mallet, giving the clothes body and a lustrous sheen.) This grinder has a broader bottom stone, and there are grooves cut into the upper surface of the bottom stone to allow only the finely ground flour to escape.

Also on Cheju Island is the king of millstones. It is so big and heavy it takes four people to turn it.

Mother-of-Pearl Inlay
나전 Najon

Inlay is one of several kinds of lacquerware craft; it is the technique in which the mother-of-pearl is cut and laid in a pattern in wood or in the lacquer surfacing on the wood.

It is not certain where or how this kind of inlay first developed, but it is known that it was a thriving industry during T'ang China (seventh to tenth centuries). They generally used wood from the southern provinces and clam shells from the South Sea, so one may surmise that the art originated in Southern China. It is believed that Koreans took up the craft of inlay in the Three Kingdoms period (first to seventh centuries A.D.), which corresponds to T'ang China. The craft reached its peak during Song China (tenth to thirteenth centuries), but then went into decline during the same dynasty. In the period of its decline in China, however, the industry flourished in Koryo dynasty Korea and Japan. Inlay, along with pottery, is a prominent art of the Koryo period.

The craft suffered a decline during the Japanese occupation, from the turn of this century until 1945. It did not die out completely, however, and enjoyed a revival after liberation in 1945. Then, with the arrival of an unprecedented period of prosperity in 1960, traditional designs started to reflect modern tastes, and became more detailed and ornate.

Oriental Medicine
한약 Hanyak

Hanyak is often referred to as Chinese medicine, because it was systematized by the Chinese in their Han dynasty (third century B.C. to third century A.D.). It is also often referred to as herbal medicine, but that is not entirely correct, since acupuncture and finger-pressure therapy are also used, and the ingredients of the medicines are not always herbal. Though herbs are the most commonly used ingredient, minerals and sometimes certain elements from animals are also used. Whether plant, mineral or animal, though, the medicines are always composed of purely natural elements.

The prescriptions used are almost always based on the traditional theory of Chinese medicine. This theory, in turn, is based on the principles of oriental philosophy. The theory comes also from an active kind of external observation of the living creature, and the basic purpose is preservation and maintenance of the interior organs of the body. Western medicine, on the contrary, is based on scientific analysis of cellular composition, and has more the feature of defending from and eliminating those elements which threaten us from the exterior. Oriental medicine, therefore, puts emphasis on active observation and prevention, while Western medicine emphasizes passive observation and treatment.

While the science has actually been practiced over the last four thousand years, it did not arrive in Korea until the early years of the Shilla dynasty.

Pillow Ends
베갯모 Begaetmo

There are all different kinds of pillows, of all different qualities, but there is hardly a Korean home without the traditional pillow. It is not the pillow itself which is so important, though—it is the pillow ends. The Korean pillow is cylindrical, providing a round, flat surface which invites the most creative embroidery art.

For the last few centuries Korean women, knowing that wishes are realized through the right kind of dreams, gave a lot of time and devotion to embroidering the pillow's ends. In these pillow ends from days past we can see our ancestors' spirit of making even the most mundane household object beautiful.

And here we can also see many of the customs of old. In the patterns of these pillow ends, for instance, are designs which show how the female mentality in those days combined orthodox Confucianism with unorthodox shamanism. "The more male offspring the better" was the orthodox Confucian principle, and having an auspicious dream was the unorthodox way of achieving this goal.

Pipe
담뱃대 Dambaetdae

In Korea the principle rule of pipe smoking is, "the longer the shank, the mellower the smoke." And so it is that the Korean pipe has a longer stalk and a smaller bowl than the western pipe.

This pipe is not only Korean, of course. It is native to the Far East, including China and Japan. Tobacco was introduced to Korea around the beginning of the seventeenth century, and the pipe came into use throughout the country within just a few years.

In the folk paintings of the eighteenth century artist Kim Hong-do we often see a member of the gentry with a long pipe in his hands. There are two kinds of traditional pipe, though, one long and one short. Originally there was only the long pipe, used exclusively by the gentry. But commoners wanted to use the pipe, too. To do something that the gentry did would be violating the Confucian mores of the time, however, so to avoid any appearance of presumptuousness, the commoners shortened the long pipe into one they could safely use. Over the years the stalk on this pipe was shortened to a degree that it could fit in one's pocket.

These days, with the disappearance of the gentry, the long pipe is no longer in regular use.

Quilt
이불 Ibul

Mention of the quilt as we know it first appears in the fifty-volume chronicle of a Chinese envoy sent by Sung China (tenth to thirteenth centuries) to the Korean court during the Koryo dynasty. The Chinese characters for "quilt" were, literally, "embroidered bedding" and "sleeping wear." Unfortunately, the pictures in this voluminous report, which would have given us a better idea of that age, have been lost: only the text remains.

A catalog on bedding was compiled in the Chosun dynasty (fourteenth to twentieth centuries); this was a very detailed depiction of what people at that time used for bedding. Another source of information about bedding is yet another catalog which described around one thousand articles of bedding used by the king. In this catalog we are provided with a full description of the magnificent colors and fabrics of King Sunjong's bedding. This book, by the way, was written on elegant Chinese paper of red, yellow, green, indigo, and pink.

These days, with our special concern for leisure, we regard bedding not only as something to keep us warm. We want it to be easy to keep clean, and it must be cozy and refreshing at the same time. It must also be aesthetically pleasing since the growing popularity of beds has made the quilt an adjunct of furniture—the bed, after all, is not folded up and put away in the closet in the morning, like traditional bedding. All sorts of materials have been developed to satisfy the growing number of functions which the quilt is expected to perform.

Rafters
서까래 Sokkarae

The roof of a Korean building usually resembles the roof of a pagoda. To form the length of this kind of roof, curved log rafters are attached, parallel to one another, to the ridgepole. Instead of using nails we cut slots in the logs and join the logs together naturally. A webbing of wood slats is attached to the rafters, and over this webbing is applied a red clay. Earthenware roof tiles are placed on this clay.

At the ends of some traditional buildings an apron of shorter rafters is appended. Another type of traditional structure has a roof which originates at a central point and radiates down and outward, resulting in a generally circular effect.

Rice Cake
떡 Ddok

What is generally called rice cake in English translation is usually made from either glutinous or non-glutinous rice, but can also be made from other grains. No matter what it is made of, it is always served at such rites of passage as the celebration of a baby's one-hundredth day, the child's first birthday, weddings, a person's sixtieth birthday, and funerals; it also appears at such traditional holiday celebrations as lunar New Year and Harvest Moon Festival. Any really special occasion calls for rice cake.

Both regional recipes and the family's circumstances determine what grain is used, with the result that there is a great variety of these cakes. Basically, however, the flour from the grain is dampened and steamed, mixed with a little water, kneaded into dough, and formed into its final shape. Then it is steamed again.

If it is not eaten on the clay it is made it begins to lose some of its freshness. Cakes left over to the next day are toasted in a light oil on a skillet.

Rice Chest
뒤주 Duiju

This household item stores any grain, from rice to beans to cereals. The best wood for it comes from the pagoda tree. Thick, solid pieces of wood are put together over four stocky legs with squat feet. We open it by lifting the hinged top. The hinges and trimmings are usually either of cast iron or bronze, but some other materials are occasionally used. A rice chest usually holds one or two sacks; some smaller grain chests hold from one-and-a-half to two gallons.

The grandaddy of all rice chests is preserved in the west coast province of North Cholla; it is made from the wood of the pagoda tree, and can hold around seventy large sacks of rice. It is one of those historic remains which reflect something of the wealth and power of the great families during the Chosun dynasty.

Rice Paddy
논 Non

The rice paddy consists of a firm bed and surrounding levees of packed earth. Cut into the levee is one sluice which lets in the water and another sluice which drains it. The type of paddy used—wet or dry—is determined by how well it drains. In the dry paddy drainage is good and its top soil is deep; it has good permeability and even if a large amount of compost is spread on the field it does not lose its oxygen. Because of this its yield is healthy and plentiful. The dry paddy in the southern parts of Korea can be double-cropped with cereal grains after the rice harvest.

The wet paddy does not drain well, which causes the soil to lose its supply of oxygen relatively soon. This kind of paddy, therefore, is not as high in yield as the dry paddy, and double-cropping is difficult.

Though rice is cultivated in some parts of North America it is most commonly cultivated between the latitudes 51° north and 35° South, in thirty countries mainly located in Southeast Asia and the Far East.

Scissors
가위 Kawi

The oldest scissors found in China are from the early Han period, in the third century B.C. Scissors have existed in the West since the age of Hellenism. They were mostly made of iron, with only a few of bronze. Hellenism's scissors, found buried in the graves of male corpses, are surmised to have been used for cutting the beard, and the scissors discovered among the historical remains of Rome are thought to have been used for cutting wire.

In the East, the oldest scissors were found in a tomb in Loyang, front the end of the earlier Han period. It is still to be determined whether scissors were invented by the Chinese or brought to China from the West. The latter possibility is suggested by the fact that scissors first appeared in the West, and both the East's and the West's share similar basic features.

Because of the form, material and use of the earliest scissors found in Korea, prior to the Three Kingdoms era in the first to seventh centuries, the guess is that they came from China. Korea introduced scissors to Japan.

Shoes
신발 Shinbal

While the shoe serves the various functions of protection, ornamentation, and facilitating certain kinds of work, ornamentation, according to historical records, was far from the mind of most people in ancient times. In those days it was only the privileged class that could wear shoes with any attention to style. Commoners, when they ventured into the wilderness, when the weather was inclement, and any time they needed protection for their feet, had to use something provided by nature, such as bark, vines or hide. The place of manufacture and the social rank of a shoe's wearer could easily be identified by the shoe's design and material.

From the beginning shoes have always been made from straw, fabric or leather, but recently synthetic materials are often used to make shoes of coordinated colors.

Sickle
낫 Nat

This implement developed along with the growth of agriculture in the neolithic age in China. In the East rice was first cut with a sickle which had a cutting edge made of stone. Soon, though, the rice culture of southern Asia came up with a cutting edge made of the rim of the clam shell. Then the process of iron casting was developed,

and it was not long before the first iron blade was formed. When the metal blade was invented part of it was bent back to form a handle set at an obtuse angle to the blade.

The sickle was referred to as a millet chisel, fingernail sickle, and other terms. The fingernail sickle was actually designed differently from the iron sickle; it retained the form of the old stone sickle. It was used for cutting the kernels of rice from the stalk. The metal sickle was used to cut the stalk itself. These two were used in tandem to revolutionize agriculture.

Skirt
치마 Chima

The traditional dress, still worn quite often by women today, has been in Korea several centuries. The same dress can be seen in paintings of women from Sung dynasty China (tenth to thirteenth centuries), so it may be presumed that this dress originated in China. While the traditional woman's dress in China changed long ago, the Korean dress retains the original design.

This dress worn by Korean women has been referred to over the centuries in many terms. One term commonly used in the fifteenth century (found in a Chinese character primer which employed everyday objects as examples to teach the characters) is still being used in several of the provinces today.

In Korean the skirt is used to describe a certain type of male: "He likes anything in a skirt." Both "the awesome swish of the skirt" and "the ubiquitous swish of the skirt" are variations of a term used when a female meddles in an unbecoming way in affairs outside the home.

Spoon and Chopsticks
수저 Sujo

From the earliest times Koreans have always used a combination of something to scoop with and something to pick up with. Before the metal spoon and chopstick came along, the shell of a clam was probably used for a spoon and two

pieces of wood for chopsticks. Since the discovery of smelting, nickel, bronze, gold, silver and other metals have been used to make the spoon and chopsticks.

Most Koreans use the spoon for eating their rice and chopsticks for side dishes, though there are some who think it proper to use the spoon only for soup.

Tadumi
다듬이질 Tadumijil

One way to smooth out clothes, of course. is with an iron. Another way to do it is the traditional Korean way, *tadumi*.

There are actually two ways of doing it in Korea. One is the simple way. by folding the clothing and placing it on a firm, hard base, then pummeling it with the laundry bat, then refolding it and going through the entire process several times. Another way is with the *hongduggae*, which is a planed and smoothed birch log seven to eight centimeters (approximately three inches) thick in the center and tapered slightly at both ends. The clothing is wrapped around the *hongduggae*, which is placed on a stand, and the clothing is beaten with the bat. The clothing on its *hongduggae* turns on the stand as the bat pounds it.

A sticky substance made from rice flour and water is sometimes applied to the clothes. After the substance is applied it is absorbed evenly into the fibers of the clothing, which is then beaten with the bat. When clothes are done this way not only are the wrinkles smoothed out, but the clothing also takes on a soft sheen.

The tranquil image and rhythmical sounds produced by *tadumi* are something unique to Korea.

Taeguk
태극 Taeguk

The Korean flag is the only national flag whose design is based on a philosophical theme rather than one that symbolizes national character. The flag takes its name, the "Taeguk flag," from the principle which it depicts. In the center is the *taeguk*, with its blue yin comma and red yang comma nestling together head to toe; this signifies the basic principle of all existence. The *taeguk* is surrounded by four trigrams of diametric but complementary arrangements of parallel lines. One trigram has three parallel solid (yang) lines, and its corresponding trigram, on the opposite side of the *taeguk*, has three parallel broken (yin) lines in the middle. The arrangement of the lines in the other two trigrams is based on the same principle of diametric complementation. These combinations of lines are extensions of the basic yin-yang principle to all things in life. The basic principle and its extension are expounded in the *Book of Changes*, where sixty-four hexagrams are used to give a detailed depiction of the composition of the universe.

Taekwondo
태권도 Taekwon

Taekwondo is an original creation of Koreans. It originated two thousand years ago as a martial art practiced by nobility and gentry, and now, in the twenty-first century, is a popular and officially recognized sport throughout the world. Taekwondo is unlike many other sports in that, as it incorporates both a martial spirit and a spirit of sport, it is the source of the integrity and dignity essential in making a fully developed person. It is also a source of physical and mental health.

Almost as soon as man first set foot on this earth he was fighting with his neighbor. When he did not have a weapon he had to use his fists or feet. Taekwondo originated in man's need to protect himself and his tribe. As civilization developed so did a moral sense in man, and along with that a system of morals. Taekwondo changed with the development of this system of morals; more emphasis was put on the mental and spiritual qualities of the practicer than on his technical skills. Out of that developed an educational function, with the result today that it is used as a

discipline for instilling a sense of morality into and refining the personalities of the young who study it.

Thimble
골무 Kolmu

The thimble originated in China some 4,500 years ago, with the first use of silk. At that time a needle approximately one-fourth the size of today's needle was used. Korea's oldest thimble comes from a burial mound of the first century B.C., in the southwestern part of North Korea.

Tiger
호랑이 Horangi

The tiger is the largest member of the cat family; the Siberian male can measure over three meters in length and weigh more than three hundred kilograms. The tiger's first home was in eastern Siberia, Manchuria and northeastern Korea; but about ten thousand years ago he crossed the Himalayan range and spread throughout warmer climates as far south as India and the Malaysian Peninsula. The farther into tropical countries the tiger progressed, the smaller his size became.

Distinguishing colors of the Korean tiger are on the back, which verges on orange, and the legs, which are closer to pure yellow. On the back are black stripes, but there are no stripes toward the front of the animal. The fur on his neck, belly and the inside of his legs is white, and on the tail are eight or nine round spots; at the end of the tail are two coal-black spots.

To the Korean the tiger, not the lion, is king of beasts. He is known variously as the sacred beast or the divine beast, and appears as the main character in many legends and folk tales. In this literature he is characterized as having a deep sense of integrity, and he has a congenial expression, somewhat in contrast to reality. The tiger of folklore seems to reflect the Korean mentality, and is therefore especially revered by Koreans.

Totem Couple
장승 Changsung

While most of Korea's guardian totems are of wood, there are also some carved from rock. They often served as boundary markers or mileposts, but in times of adversity, such as political turmoil or plague. most have doubled as divine protectors. It is hard to find them these days, but In the old days they were posted at every willage entrance and every temple gate.

Various hypotheses exist its to their origin. One proposes they may have begun as phallic symbols, erected for women to pray to for either the birth of a male or for virility in the male who was not performing. Another hypothesis suggests that they may have originated as something to mark the boundary of the government-subsidized farm of a Buddhist temple. (The Chosun dynasty, which fostered Confucianism as a state system of thought, ceased this subsidization in its effort to hinder the development and lessen the influence of Buddhism.)

Another opinion is that the first wood totems were erected to enlist the help of supernatural powers in such important matters as the *kwago* (all examination administered in the selection of candidates for high government office) or the harvest, and that only the stone totem had its beginning as a phallic symbol.

Tripitaka Koreana
팔만대장경 Palmandaejangkyong

The first edition of this gigantic enterprise was a result partly of efforts at helping Buddhism flourish, but this highly civilized country also had another purpose, that of protecting the country at a critical point in its history and enhancing its power vis-a-vis its neighbors through the intercession of Buddha. This set of classics was begun at the time of the Mongol invasion and took 240 years of the nation's concerted effort to get completely into print. Once it was in print, though, it was obvious that it not only accomplished the purpose of gaining respect for the country from its adversaries Sung China and

Manchuria, this endeavor also contributed much to the development of printing and publishing.

Trousers
바지 Baji

Korea's first written record of a word similar to the current word used for trousers is found in the writings of a scholar of the early Chosun dynasty, around the fifteenth century. He used two Chinese characters, pronounced in Korean as *pa* (hold, tie, or keep) and *ji* (hold). The currently used word is *baji*. In the middle Chosun dynasty, around the eighteenth century, the aspirated *paji* was used in reference to the lower clothing worn at a state marriage and court ceremonies. The trousers worn by the king and queen, though, were not referred to in the same term as that used for the trousers worn by his subjects. (Many other words are reserved specially for use in reference to the king or queen.)

Korean men's trousers have changed but slightly over the last millennium. During the transition from the Koryo dynasty to the Chosun dynasty (around 1400) they changed slightly to take on the form currently in use. Women in the Three Kingdoms period (first to seventh centuries) used to wear trousers even for formal wear, but after they took to wearing the long skirt the trousers came to be worn as inner garments.

Walls
담 Dam

Walls in Korea range from the simple wicket fence to the stronger stone, brick and cinder block walls.

The entirety of old Seoul was surrounded by a wall of earth faced with heavy stone. This wall, sections of which remain even today, was built at the end of the fourteenth century, when the Chosun dynasty established Seoul as the nation's capital. It was about sixteen kilometers long, enclosing what was then all of Seoul but is now the very heart of the twentieth-century megapolis which sprawls miles beyond the wall. The wall

had nine gates, situated according to the principles of geomancy. (The site of the capital itself was selected and laid out in accordance with these principles). Five of these gates exist today and are maintained as historical properties.

A branch of this main wall, recently restored, was built in the eighteenth century. It extends over eight kilometers, from the West Gate to a pass in one of the mountains north of the city. Another wall, outside of the city, was built to protect the eastern approach to the capital: it is seven meters high and seven kilometers in length. Erection of the wall began in the seventeenth century; like the wall which protects the northern and western approaches to the city. Much of it is being maintained today.

Wardrobe
장농 Jangnong

With that great variety of clothing worn in a country with four seasons there has to be a suitable place to store it all, and the traditional wardrobe does the job. The whole year's clothing is always at hand, but the current season's clothing is even more at hand—right on top.

We have two kinds of wardrobe, which comprise a set generically referred to the *jangnong*. The *jang* has two or more compartments stacked on top of each other, and the *nong* has these compartments with the addition of a side compartment or two. The modern wardrobe has a space for hanging clothing on hangers.

Just as in centuries past it is the responsibility of the new bride to provide the *jangnong* set for the new household. The wardrobe is still one of the central pieces of any household, and is therefore usually a quite elaborate affair of mother-of-pearl inlay.

Water Mill
물레방아 Mullebanga

The water mill is usually not erected on the banks of a river or stream; a separate tributary is excavated for it.

The more primitive water mill consisted mainly of a large log with a pestle attached to the bottom of one end. At the other end of this log a receptacle was carved out to catch the water diverted from the river or stream. When the receptacle filled with water that end of the log went down, raising the other end. The water spilled out when the receptacle went down low enough, and the released weight allowed the end with the pestle, now the heavier of the two ends, to crash down on the grain awaiting its fate lit the mortar. Meanwhile the receptacle at the other end began filling again with water.

The more advanced water mill is the one with the water wheel, which we still find on occasion in both the West and in Korea. It is of a more complex construction and operation than the ordinary person would suspect. The wheel shaft, an extension of the axle, is a wide board which is turned round and round by the water wheel; this shaft, as it turns, will meet the end of a beam to which the pestle is fixed at its other end. It forces the contact end down, thus raising the pestle end. When the shaft turns a bit further it releases its hold on the pestle beam, and the pestle end then plunges down, crushing the grain in the mortar.

Wicker Basket
바구니 Bakuni

It appears that this portly, bottomless basket made of bamboo strips or the stem of the bush clover has been used since the neolithic age, and was certainly in use in Egypt more than five thousand years ago.

In Korea the wicker basket of Tamyang, in South Cholla Province, is considered to be best in quality. The delicately woven, brightly colored wicker basket is one of Korea's most popular handicraft exports.

The Wind Bell
풍경 Pungkyong

This is usually hung on the roof's hip in temples

and pavilions. It is actually a small temple bell, with the addition of a clapper inside and a wafer-thin wind catcher of bronze in the form of a carp. The captured wind works with the clapper and bell to produce a wistful, solitary sound of crystal clarity. The wind chime was transmitted to Korea from China long ago, so we can easily imagine our Korean ancestors, like the characters in so many Chinese ink paintings from that time, sitting on a breezy veranda and letting the wind bell stir their poetic sentiments.

The Winnow
키 Ki

These days in Korea and almost every other industrialized nation the combine does our winnowing for us. When a small winnowing job comes up we have to look for something laying around the yard that can serve as a makeshift tray because there are no more hand winnowers. The old hand winnower is valued more as an antique than as an implement.

Wrapper
보 Bo

This four-cornered wrapper used to be assembled from scraps of cloth, with the result that it would be difficult to find two that looked alike. In bygone days it was used to cover and wrap anything and everything, which explains why it has so many different sizes. There was the huge wrapper for storing and transporting quilts, the smaller wrapper used its a dust cover for the side dishes on the table set for dinner, the yet smaller one to store and carry personal accessories, and the wrapper to hold letters. Each of these had its own name, which identified either how the wrapper was used or what the wrapper was made of. There was the embroidered wrapper, the scraps wrapper, and many others.

Depending on its function, it could be a one-ply or a two-ply wrapper. The one for covering or wrapping food was lined with oil paper.

The wrapper used by the bride to bundle up her quilt when she moved in with her husband's family was usually of a peach colored linen; a popular theme for decoration was an imprint of a water chestnut blossom woodblock print, which was displayed on the top when the bride folded it up and put it away after moving in with her new family.

The wrapper of today is most often made of synthetic materials.

Wrestling
씨름 Ssirum

Two men put their heads over each other's left shoulder, grab the thigh band wrapped around shoulder, legs thick as tree trunks, and at a signal from the referee throw every bit of their skill and muscle into dumping the other onto the ground. In primitive times they practiced in this way to make themselves fit for life-or-death struggles with other tribes and wild beasts. But when society turned to agriculture this indigenous form of wrestling became it form of entertainment to accompany the performance of ceremonial rites on traditional holidays such as the Harvest Moon Festival.

Korea was an agricultural society and venerated agriculture as the most respectable occupation one could have, apart from scholar or statesman. So agriculture was promoted in every way possible. At the larger wrestling contests a bull was given as grand prize as a way of encouraging men to grow strong so they could work hard and produce more. They also expected the winner to use his prize in the field to contribute to even more agricultural production.

Yut
윷놀 Yut

This board game was invented in Korea, and has been played here since before the Three Kingdoms period, which began in the first century A. D.

It is a long-standing tradition to play this game from lunar New Year to about the fifteenth of the first lunar month. The nature of this game is quite indicative of the Korean character; it often gets quite raucous but never loses its basic wholesomeness.

Normally the game is played by two or three players, though when there are more the game is played in teams. There are twenty-nine spots on the board, and each player has four pieces to move over these spots before one's opponents do. First, four sticks, flat on the face and rounded on the bottom, are thrown to determine the order of play: once this has been determined the sticks are thrown again by one player to determine the number of spaces the player can move ahead. If all four sticks land face down, the player advances five places; all four face up sends the player ahead four places. Two up and two down allow the player to move two ahead, three up and one down move the player three steps, and one up and three down advance the player only one. The first player to get all his pieces through the gate at the end of the board wins.